FINDING
WORK
you
LOVE

FINDING WORK YOU LOVE

3 STEPS TO GETTING THE PERFECT JOB AFTER COLLEGE

KIRK SNYDER

TEN SPEED PRESS

California | New York

Contents

For Mom, Dad, and W—*my angels*

Introduction

Why Success After College Is *All About You*

There are all kinds of career resources out there, including books, blogs, websites, and seminars, as well as an ocean of tests designed to spit out job titles that are supposedly just right for you. Maybe you've seen them; they often talk about how to *dream big, find your true calling*, or *write a winning resume*. But even with all of this available information, millions of college students graduate each year into unemployment, underemployment, or, often, a job they hate. Instead of launching into careers after college that generate choruses of "Yes, this is why I went to college!" or "This makes all of my hard work and sacrifice worth it!," many students end up thinking: "Maybe I should go back to graduate school and get into even more debt," or "Maybe I will just take any job for now and figure it out later," or, in my opinion, the saddest thought of all: "I don't know where to look, so I'm not even going to try."

Unfortunately, these last three choruses seem to be getting louder and louder each year. And it isn't just at the undergraduate level; graduate students are adrift in the same murky sea. It seems to be less about the economy flourishing or languishing and more about understanding how to systematically connect who you are to what you do based on the realities of any current job market. It's a sad professional reality for what I believe is an amazing and ambitious generation of talent (that's you!).

As a professor at USC's Marshall School of Business, I've watched my own students struggle with this postgraduation dilemma for years. This is why I was motivated to create a new career class for undergraduates that was much more tangible and practical than simply dreaming big or finding your one true calling. I wanted to help them better figure out who they are, but in a way that each student could effectively use to level the playing field in what is ultimately a very new world of work (more on this later).

I wanted to focus my class more on the discovery of each student's individual value and how that value actually plays into *finding work you love* than on resume writing or interviewing. As part of my research to develop and refine the information that would serve as the foundation of this class, I started talking to people about their jobs. On planes, in restaurants, or with guest speakers in the classroom, whenever I encountered someone who said they loved their job and couldn't imagine doing anything else, I asked this question: "Why do you love your job, and what do you bring to the table that makes you successful doing what you're doing?" Fortunately, people who love what they do also love talking about it, and so the "ingredients" of what goes into finding work you love in today's landscape started to get really clear.

I also noticed that a very small group of college students—and maybe you know some of these people—do graduate with jobs they love. Perhaps it's not surprising, but as I followed the careers of these students after college, I saw that they also seemed to quickly get raises and promotions. But here's what *was* surprising, at least to me. The students I knew who had found that elusive right fit job aren't necessarily more driven or talented than the majority of students who didn't find it. While the happy students who graduated into jobs they love were definitely driven and talented, the positive force behind their right fit didn't appear to be about IQ, EQ, GPAs, or majors—and it definitely wasn't about writing a perfect resume.

Grounded in all of the information I was gathering, I knew there *had* to be a way to create a system that all students could use based on what that small happy group of students had done, either knowingly or unknowingly, to find their super-satisfying job, because I could see how similar their positive outcomes were across very different fields. The career system I wanted for my students would be fueled by the positive force created when *who they are* and *what they do* come together in a specific and powerful way. This was unquestionably the key to why that small group of happy students was having a wildly different professional outcome than the majority of their classmates. And because that small happy group was composed of very different people with very different interests and backgrounds, I knew the system could be personalized for *all students*. After all, as I was learning, finding a right-fit job is about more than just having a job. It is personal, and it is *all about you*.

What you're getting ready to read about, the Working *You* system, represents the specific ingredients that go into finding work you love. Over several years, they have been refined through on-the-ground practice that included trial, error, student feedback, and my own research studying the real-life career experiences of college graduates across the country, happy and unhappy, to figure out what was creating that positive force behind their right fit. What I found when all of the puzzle pieces were finally put together is a system that explains how you can be rewarded for the value that you alone bring to today's all-new job market. And it's not just about finding *one* job. I absolutely believe there are many right fits out there for everyone, including you, which you will soon discover for yourself.

In varying degrees, every job will either reward or punish you for the collective value you bring to an employer. If you're "working *you*," you're being rewarded for the value you uniquely offer. This is a system that doesn't rely on luck or serendipity or fate—it just relies on you. It is also an *open system* and therefore adaptable to individual circumstances and flexible to change over time. The Working *You* system will provide you with your own custom step-by-step blueprint to go out and create the exact same type of powerful and rewarding right fit that small happy group of new graduates who love their jobs are experiencing. (And with this book, I believe that group is about to get bigger.)

As I brought the Working *You* system to my own students, I began to see that it was making a real difference. Based on student demand, the decision was made to quickly expand this class and offer multiple sections, and then we doubled the number of seats per section. I was then asked to create a parallel class for MBA students, who were also struggling to find a right fit. Similar to the experience of the undergraduate class, word of mouth among the graduate students resulted in a waiting list long enough to fill another whole class, which we did. At that point, I knew I was breaking the code to at least one system that all students could personalize for themselves to find a right-fit job after college across both undergraduate and graduate programs.

Creating a Positive Force

For anyone who has taken an introductory physics course, you know that Sir Isaac Newton believed in a special kind of action and reaction that occurs when two objects make contact. Newton said that when objects A and B interact, the contact between these two separate objects generates its own force. That's exactly what is happening for students who graduate into jobs they love.

It wasn't until one of my students casually referenced Newton in a classroom discussion completely unrelated to the topic of jobs that I started to consider how, in a right fit, the *action* and *reaction* Newton talked about was analogous to the action of students bringing their own collective value to an employer and the reaction of an employer either rewarding or punishing them for that value. In a right fit, being rewarded for the value you bring to the job ignites a positive force between you and your job. In a bad fit, there isn't enough energy to ignite this force.

As it turns out, finding a right fit that will reward you for who you are at work isn't the great mystery it seems to be—as long as you have the right ingredients connected together in the right way. And, by the way, the "ingredients" don't have anything to do with who you know or where you go to school. The key ingredients consist of three very specific points of value, each made up of unique attributes that you already possess. The other three ingredients consist of correlating points that will result in the employer rewarding or not rewarding your value. At the end of the day, finding work you love is really all about the powerful force of working *you*.

The Power of Intrinsic Motivation

Intrinsic motivation means doing a job that makes you feel good about yourself because it matters—*to you*. It means going to work and giving your all because you care about your job and your employer cares about you. It means that your talents fuel your job performance in ways that serve as the wind at your back. It means you are proud to tell people what you do and where you do it. *It means your human value, functional value, and image value are being rewarded by your employer.*

I'm sure you've heard the advice to "find your passion" about a million and a half times from a million and a half different people. One day I asked my students how many of them have been told to *find their passion*. Of course, everyone raised their hand. Just between us, I've grown to really dislike this advice—not because the people who tell you to find your passion aren't well-meaning; they are. But for a lot of students, the search to find their passion sounds very open-ended and from the outside can appear to be driven by chance and luck. One of my students told me that, for her, this advice conjures up images of getting all dressed up in her best business suit and wandering through her city's financial district, then past the hospitals and health care companies, then over to the movie and entertainment studios, and finally, on to the technology and arts districts—any section of town where businesses of a like nature hub up. All the while, she is hoping to bump into her *passion*, which she said she would clearly recognize by the sound of harps playing as the heavens opened up the moment they collided. It just doesn't happen that way. The passion that everyone tells you to find is simply what I believe is intrinsic motivation. From an experiential perspective, I've found them to be the same thing. Fortunately, you can create intrinsic motivation because it is indeed tangible and generated by that positive force between you and your job. *This book is all about helping you find it.*

About This Book

It was perhaps fortuitous that, as I was writing this introduction, one of my Working *You* students wrote the following comment on the end-of-semester course evaluation I'm sure many of you have filled out in your own classes: "Professor Snyder has made a seemingly daunting task doable by breaking it up into bite-sized pieces." Finding a job where you will be rewarded for who you are should not cause pain or confusion—starting with your first job after college and the job after that, and the one after that.

My best recommendation for you to maximize the value of this book is to read each step in order, without skipping ahead. Otherwise, you risk leaving out some of the richness of each ingredient, and that could make a big difference in your custom blueprint to finding work you love. I think you'll discover that the process of finding your right-fit job is clearly laid out in three easy-to-follow steps (briefly outlined for you below). Trust in the building process of each step, and at the end of the book you'll be in exactly the right place.

Step One (chapters 1–5) is all about defining your three specific points of unique professional value that I call You Points. I define these as your *human value*, *functional value*, and *image value*. Collectively, they represent the tremendous worth you offer to employers in today's job market.

Step Two (chapters 6–9) provides you with your own personalized job bank, populated with twenty-five potential right fits tailor-made for you. This step steers you toward fields, companies, and roles in which there is a strong and authentic connection between who you are and what you do that will produce the energy you need to ignite that positive force.

Step Three (chapters 10–11) is all about creating your custom blueprint to turn those right fits into job offers. This stage of the process takes you *to and through* that well-hidden gateway where that happy group of new graduates who love their jobs live their professional lives.

As you progress through each of the three steps, you'll meet a very diverse and interesting group of people to help bring the process to life. Some are recent graduates from colleges all around the United States, while others are more seasoned professionals. Metaphorically, and perhaps practically, these people will serve as your own team of career advisors, helping you gain as much clarity as possible as you use the system to find and secure your own right fit.

I've also included some completed templates that illustrate how to tailor the Working *You* system uniquely for you. These personal templates will bring each step to life through two students, Cara and Sam. Unlike the other people you'll meet along the way, Cara and Sam aren't real people. They are composites of many students I know (see sidebar) and are presented as current college students to model how to complete each step of the system. My goal for using student models is to provide you with a how-to resource to make personalizing the system both user-friendly and stress-free. If you follow the steps of their progression, using their completed templates as examples, you will wind up at your desired destination at the end of the book—just like Cara and Sam do.

Who Are Cara and Sam?

Cara and Sam are the combination of thousands of undergraduate and graduate students I have had in my own classes or interviewed specifically for this book. By using this method of personal consolidation to create these two student models, my hope is that you can recognize some part of yourself in one or perhaps both of them as you walk down the same path. By following Cara and Sam, you never have to worry about taking a wrong turn or getting off track.

Final Words

The outcome I'm seeking for you is to have you singing the first two choruses I mentioned at the beginning of the introduction:

"Yes, this is why I went to college!"

"This makes all of my hard work and sacrifice worth it!"

Before we get started, you should know that in addition to all of the people you will meet in the pages of this book, I am your advisor too. I believe in you, and I believe in the value you bring to today's job market. I've seen droves of students who didn't recognize their value, or didn't think of themselves as special or deserving, begin to see themselves through a new lens as a result of going through the steps you are about to take. Open yourself up to all of the possibilities that are out there for you and *believe in yourself*.

Now, let's do this.

STEP ONE

• •

Defining Your Unique Value in the Job Market

• •

"Success is a science; if you have the conditions, you get the results."
—Oscar Wilde

Everyone who meets and spends some quality time with Thomas Tran would agree that he's incredibly smart—and funny. He's someone you like immediately. Thomas is the person his friends often reach out to for career advice because he cares—and because he has walked a very interesting professional path that has led to that happy destination where he is richly rewarded for the value he brings to the world of work. What his friends typically hear is career advice that, admittedly, he didn't always follow himself. "Find what makes you feel good as a human being, and you will be headed in the right direction."

Thomas went to the University of California at Berkeley for his undergraduate degree, majoring in literature, and then went on to graduate from Stanford Law. He practiced at a top fifty law firm right out of law school, moved to another firm in search of a better culture, and by the age of thirty-two, became general counsel at a $3 billion company. "At the beginning of my career, I looked for jobs simply based on practicality and the paycheck, and I hated going to work."

Born just seven weeks after his family arrived in the United States following the fall of Vietnam, Thomas symbolized a new life for his family and the opportunity to work hard and become successful. "In my family, taking your foot off the pedal was never an option." In junior high Thomas was student body president. In high school he was editor in chief of the school paper. "I was always turned on by story, whether fiction, histories, or journalism, and that led me to declare literature as my major at Berkeley. I loved the experience of reading or watching films, and I was passionate about learning how storytellers strategically approached their work. How they expressed things was just as important as what they expressed."

Thomas describes his time at Berkeley as "four of the best years of my life. I felt free and alive and engaged." During a one-year stint as a Fulbright scholar to study literature in Vietnam immediately after college, he applied to and was accepted into the UCLA film school, which was the creative path he wanted to follow. But the pull of familial duty also led him to "cover his bases" and take the LSATs: "When I was growing up, Asian American kids were not encouraged to pursue anything creative. In fact, we were discouraged. It may occur less so today, but I doubt much less. Career pragmatism is simply part of the culture."

Thomas applied to Stanford Law School and, based on the strength of his essay, he got in. After a deep struggle with making a life-changing decision at this professional crossroads, he went to law school and put his creative path on hold. Thomas says he felt like a "different species" from his classmates. "My performance was totally different than it had been at Berkeley, because I wasn't really connected to the material. You have to be connected to the material." But he kept his foot on the pedal and graduated from law school and into a good job market and a good salary, but not into what he describes as "a good fit." He shared, "The creativity that drove me before just wasn't there. I needed to be with people who looked at the world through a creative lens, and a law firm wasn't that place. The money was great, but life wasn't great."

During the time in his career when "life wasn't great," Thomas's college friend and coworker from Berkeley saw how unhappy he was and made him an offer to come work with him in his new start-up. "I liked Howard's mentality about work: *Don't go to stuff that sucks.*" Thomas also admired Howard's ability to be "unburdened" by what others wanted him to do and his motivation to follow his own path. It was an ability that Thomas admits he struggled with for a long time.

While Howard's new business sounded like a great idea for Howard, Thomas knew the offer to join him wasn't a right fit either, even though he was looking for an exit from his job at a law firm. "I was tempted, really tempted. I was so unfulfilled doing what I was doing, and Howard knew I wasn't working in a way that really meant anything to me beyond a paycheck." It was nonetheless a pivotal point in Thomas's career. "Coming so close to giving up my very well-paying law career to join a start-up, which I also knew wasn't a right fit, made me realize that I needed to make a change."

Howard later sold his start-up for more than half a billion dollars. When I asked Thomas if he ever regrets not joining Howard's company, I was impressed with the level of self-awareness expressed in his answer. "If money was all that was important to me, then I would definitely have regrets. Looking back from where I am today, it's very clear that Howard's start-up wasn't right for me either. I was already making a lot of money, so that wasn't what tempted me. But I do owe Howard a debt of gratitude for calling out my wrong fit and helping me recognize that you can be rewarded in your career for taking a risk and pursuing a direction that represents your own path. In fact, it seems less risky than pursuing something you don't love."

For Thomas, finding his way back onto his own path began when he moved from a law firm to a company where the creative energy was much higher. Here, he was given the opportunity to operate with a lot more self-direction and autonomy. Being trusted to solve business problems by thinking creatively to reach results is what he attributes to actually putting him back on track. "Being true to my own abilities and interests, and more importantly, who I am as a human being, is what made the difference. Before I made the change, I actually thought I had lost my creativity. Use it or lose it. But it was still there. It was a little rusty, but as I was given more and more opportunities to draw on it, it came back full force. It was then I knew I avoided going to a bad place in my career."

After reconnecting with those same creative talents that made his four years at Berkeley the best years of his life, Thomas decided to branch out and start his own company. "Even though it had been years, I took inspiration from Howard and many others who had chosen a path that fits their unique identities and abilities."

Today, Thomas has his own legal and business advisory firm, representing what he describes as "an amazing group of clients who recognize that business is about creativity." With a client list made up of almost all entrepreneurs, Thomas picks and chooses clients who "motivate and inspire" him. "I see my clients as the catalysts of the world. I'm facilitating innovation that matters to me with people who inspire me. I am hands-on communicating with clients and understanding their stories and needs in order to help them with general business development and strategy. Of course, I use my legal experience, but what I do now goes far beyond the law, because I actually become part of the creative process with my clients. For me, creativity simultaneously motivates and inspires me every day—just like it did when I was loving my life back at Berkeley. It's really who I am and what I'm all about. I'm using my talents to generate value, and I can happily tell you I am without question on my right path. I tell my friends who ask for career advice, being true to who you are will open up the right doors because it guides you in the right direction."

As we concluded our interview, I asked him how he defines success at this point in his career. "Having control of my life in a way that allows me to define the meaning of success for me and my wife is a big part of what I actually *view as success*. I see my creativity as a source of having that control because I'm using it to my professional advantage. I'm not a billionaire, but I'm grateful we're in the top percentage of earners. But I honestly have no need to be in the top 1 percent of the top 1 percent. It's not the most important thing to me. I'm doing work that I love and making a difference in a way that makes me happy because I'm constantly using strengths that are organic to me. The biggest bonus is that I can spend time with my family and play a big role in my kids' lives. Not feeling trapped, but rather creative and vital, helps me be a fun dad. To me, that's probably the biggest benefit of how I see using my creativity: it has given me control of my life. If being happy is the definition of success, then I won."

The Visual: Working *You*

One way to think about having a job in which you are motivated and inspired to do what you do every day using abilities that are "organic" to you is to view you and your job as a system that works in harmony—where all of the key moving parts fit together in just the right way. The diagram below shows exactly what it looks like to be Working *You*.

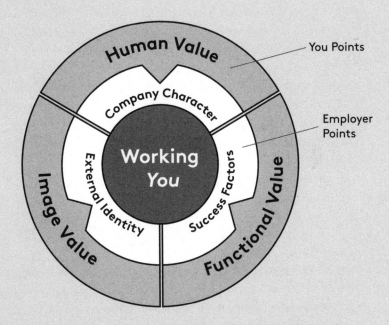

The Working *You* system itself consists of three circles. The outer circle is made up of your three individual You Points, which collectively represent those key ingredients that are the three points of value you uniquely bring to the job market.

Your Human Value

Your Functional Value

Your Image Value

Each of your You Points in the outer circle has a correlating Employer Point in the second circle. The correlating Employer Points are:

The Company Character

The Success Factors

The External Identity

When your three You Points are strategically connected to the three correlating Employer Points in a job that's a right fit, they lock together as you see in the visual. In a right fit, there's no daylight between who you are and what you do. As I said in the introduction, when you are rewarded by the employer for your own unique value—which is what's happening when the system's two outer circles are locked together—the energy between you and your job ignite the positive force that generates the core of the system, which is exactly where the commodity of intrinsic motivation exists. *It's the core of the Working* You *system*. It's also the power that will drive your professional life, now and into the future, in a happy and relevant direction.

Together, and with the help of career advisors throughout the book like Thomas, you will personalize this system uniquely for you. Yes, it can be adapted and replicated, because it is an open system. It's for this reason that I shared the Oscar Wilde quote to introduce the first step: "Success is a science; if you have the conditions, you get the results."

The Visual: *Not Working You*

It's worthwhile to quickly show you what this same system looks like when you're in a bad fit. What you see in this second diagram is a system without a core, because who you are and what you do aren't connected. There is definitely daylight between the two outer circles, and the reason the center core is nonexistent is because there isn't enough energy to generate a positive force between you and your job. Therefore, intrinsic motivation can't exist, because there's no mechanism to produce it.

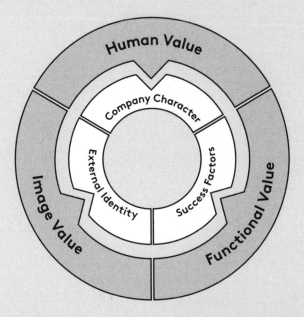

Here's a quick analogy I share with my students to describe the difference between these two situations. If you've ever tried putting furniture or an electronic toy together without reading the directions, you likely know the frustration that results when things don't fit together in the right way. Sometimes you may try to force parts together that aren't supposed to be together. Other times you may decide to leave certain parts out simply because you don't see where they fit. Either way, whatever you've built, even if it looks good for the moment on the outside, isn't sustaining, because there's no core strength to support it. And when there's no core strength, in all likelihood it's soon going to fall apart. What I know to be true from my own experience on the ground as a college professor is that the majority of new college graduates are struggling somewhere inside this second diagram—and it can truly feel like being lost.

Graduating from college is hard work. It takes dedication, perseverance, sacrifice, courage, and the fortitude to overcome a multitude of obstacles and challenges—it takes grit. And after all of that grit, you deserve to love your job. You deserve to live your best life. Whether you already have an appreciation for the value you bring to the world of work and ideas about right-fit jobs or you have no idea, be reassured that you are in exactly the right place. Finding work you love simply requires *you*, and starting in chapter 1, you will begin to see just how much value you have.

1

You Points and Why You Should Believe in Yourself

"In a nutshell, the key to success is identifying those unique modules of talent within you and then finding the right arena to use them."
—Warren Bennis

If you recognize that your You Points represent why you should believe in yourself, they will prevent you from getting lost. Your three points of value are what set you apart from everyone else in the world of work and pinpoint exactly why you have what it takes to succeed in a right fit. As we set the groundwork to define what each of these points are uniquely for you in the next three chapters, I want you to first take a moment and let this important principle of the system become entrenched.

Don't compare yourself to anyone else or wish that you were anyone other than you. Yes, aspire to grow, and aspire to discover new talents and develop new skills that will leverage those talents. Most of all, appreciate the value you possess right now as you are reading this book. Your own You Points of value represent exactly why you should believe in yourself. They are all you need to

Feeling Stressed and Scared

When I spoke with Madeleine Angiuli, she had graduated from the University of Arizona two months earlier with a double major in English and psychology. A bright and talented young woman, she was struggling with her next career steps, like millions of students all over the country.

I asked Madeleine where she was in her career path. "I feel like I'm not in control of my life and that I've done something wrong. I guess I thought it would all just work out. Once the pomp of graduation was over, there was this realization that it actually wasn't just all going to work out. I'm stressed out and scared. Right now, I'm mostly just sad."

Madeleine had recently had the worst job interview at an American-based multinational retail giant. "I received an e-mail that the company was hiring for an e-commerce position, and I immediately sent in my resume." She also sent her resume to a medical company for a sales position. "I'm feeling so stuck, but I'm also scared to death about getting stuck in a job I hate." Neither interview went anywhere, which made her feel even worse. "Getting turned down by jobs I didn't even really want, but felt like I needed, seemed a lot worse than getting turned down by jobs I wanted. I've started thinking grad school would be a great escape plan for me and that maybe I'm not really good enough to get a good job with a bachelor's degree. I honestly don't want more debt, but I just don't know."

Madeleine's experience may be your experience. When I asked her to describe what she saw as her top three talents (these factor into her Functional Value point), she seemed to welcome the question, but hadn't thought a lot about it. Once we began going down this road, exploring why she *did* have value as a new college graduate, I could sense some of the sadness starting to fade. "Creativity would be number one," she said. As we talked, I learned that she loves to write, to read a good story, and to be part of any type of creative process.

We talked about her favorite television series and what draws her into a Netflix binge, and it all seemed to circle back to writing. She loves analyzing how characters develop, how the story impacts people's emotions, and, when done really well, how good writing even has the power to change lives. From there, we did a deeper dive into her other top talents as well as her personality and what really motivates her when it comes to a job. We were essentially winding through all of her You Points. Right about this time she stopped me. "I've never thought about it this way before." I was now talking to a bright and talented young woman who was more hopeful than sad.

start your career in a powerful and rewarding way. *This is why success after college is all about you.*

If you've experienced the same feelings and fears as Madeleine (see opposite page), don't worry, we're going to figure *you* out too. First, let's look at each one of the You Points up close.

You Point #1: Your Human Value

Your Human Value is the most personal and also the most important ingredient to recognize and appreciate in the Working *You* system. Why? Because if you're not valued for who you are as a human being, no matter how hard you work or how talented you are in any given role, all of your hard work and talent won't advance the needle of success as far as it should—or as far as you deserve. If your Human Value and the Company Character of the employer in this first connection point between you and your job isn't locked into place, it can serve as a professional roadblock. Your Human Value is defined through three key attributes:

Demographics

These are the core demographic descriptors you would assign to yourself that describe you as a unique individual: for example, age, gender identification, race, cultural background, sexual orientation, and education represent these types of descriptors. In addition, any cognitive or physical realities that might impact job performance also get factored in here. It's important to note that cognitive or physical realities are not viewed as disabilities or challenges in the Working *You* system because they are not liabilities in a right fit. Rather, they are simply other important descriptors that represent the value of who you are as a human being.

Personality

These are the core traits that describe your personality. For our purposes here, I recommend the Myers-Briggs Type Indicator as one option to gain self-awareness about this second attribute of your Human Value point. It's important to identify preferences for cognitive functions that govern your energy and focus, including being an introvert or extrovert, because just as you have an original personality, every employer has an original personality too. The more self-awareness you can create for yourself around this particular ingredient, the more criteria you will have to find a job in which both "person-alities" fit. Your preferences for these cognitive functions can also play into job performance, based on what the actual role calls for you to do to perform successfully.

Motivational Work Triggers

These are the core principles that reflect what motivates you personally and professionally, identified through *intangible* triggers that are important to you—for example, integrity, ethics, providing service to others—as well as important *tangible* triggers, such as money, job security, job title, work/leisure time balance.

And that's exactly why this first fit point between your Human Value and the employer's Company Character needs to be strategically locked in. If you feel you need to *dim your light* (see opposite page), then you're not being valued for who you are as a unique individual. I love this metaphor, because every single person reading this book has their own "light." In fact, start thinking about this first You Point as your own distinctive and exclusive light.

A favorite colleague of mine who is also one of the key leaders at USC's career center advises, "Everyone is unique, and that's what you should market to employers." No matter how you define your own demographic descriptors, as well as your personality and your motivational work triggers, your Human Value point is the *source* of your other two You Points. Absolutely hold on to this foundational advice as we move ahead.

Don't Dim Your Light

When I interviewed Maura Cheeks, she was pursuing her MBA from NYU Stern School of Business. With an undergraduate degree from the University of Pennsylvania in communications and behavior, Maura has had her writing featured in the *Harvard Business Review* (*HBR*) and the *New York Times*. I was excited to talk to her because her work addresses the importance of being valued for who you are as a human being in the workplace. I had read an article she wrote for *HBR* and reached out to her because it absolutely brought to life for me the importance of this first You Point of Human Value.

Focusing on the professional experiences of African American women in a study she conducted at Stern, Maura found that when you feel as though you need to change who you are in order to fit in, you are doing yourself a tremendous disservice. In fact, doing so is referred to in her *HBR* article as the act of "dimming your light," a phrase she heard while interviewing one woman for her study. I loved our conversation about this important topic, and she offered what I believe are valuable insights and advice for all job seekers. "I think the freedom to walk comfortably in your own shoes can take a lot of different forms. For some people, it means showing up unapologetically the way you are. Meaning you don't want to separate identities between work and home—you want to be able to use each one to fuel the energy that you bring to the other. I think anytime you're made to feel like you have to shrink who you are either personally or professionally, your output is going to suffer because you won't feel safe and supported. The safer you feel at work, both physically and mentally, the more willing and able you are to bring your best self to the workplace."

You Point #2: Your Functional Value

The second You Point in the system, your Functional Value, is directly related to delivering an exemplary job performance day after day. Your Functional Value is made up of two related but distinct parts: talents and skills. I want you to think of your talents as *innate abilities* that ideally serve as the foundation for your *developed abilities*, which we are identifying here as skills. I found this alliance between talents and skills to be a key contributor to why that small group of recent college graduates who love their jobs are also quickly getting promotions and pay raises. What's the connection? Their Functional Value is being optimized through this alliance between their talents and skills to meet the Success Factors of their job—not in a mediocre way, but in an exceptional way.

What I have found in my own research is that there is basically what I call a *shared smartness* when you reach most mid-management levels. Everyone is equally smart. What catapults people upward into higher executive roles, as well as the C-suite, revolves around two primary dynamics. One is emotional intelligence, which we have known for years to be true, based on Daniel Goleman's pioneering work. The other factor, however, is a bit different. It's about building skills based on talents. When I peel the onion all the way back for those who have happily reached the highest heights in their career, they have almost always used their innate abilities—their talents—as the wind at their back to become exceptional performers.

Your Functional Value is defined through two key attributes: your talents and skills.

Talents

In the Working *You* system, talents are your *innate abilities*, and directly tied to your behavioral characteristics. In this definition, think of your talents as functional qualities that, as I already stated, can ideally serve as the wind at your back to support your job performance. Examples of talents as we are defining them range from being empathetic, detail-oriented, and methodical, to being curious and adventurous. Talents may also speak to a specialized aptitude, such as being musical, athletic, or even a gifted painter. There are an infinite number of talents that exist both in terms of behavioral characteristics as well as specialized aptitudes, and you will discover and define all of yours in chapter 3.

Skills

Skills are distinct from talents because they are defined as provable, *developed abilities*. For example, while talents are the supportive undercurrent that others can't see relative to your job performance, skills represent what's on top of the water, the outcome that others can see. Consider the bullet points on your resume as a representation of the skills you have developed based on experience gathered through classes as well as internships, part-time jobs, volunteer work, and so on. For example: Prepared daily summaries of top stock performers for analysts; Cofounded and led student entrepreneurship club; Assisted in fund-raising outreach for raising more than $100,000 for the American Cancer Society. Then, think about whether or not your talents are supporting the development of your skills. Are your talents serving as the wind at your back as you build the bullet points on your resume? Don't worry about your answer right now, or even whether you have a resume. But do think about this relationship between your talents and skills, because it is a key point of connection in the system.

Right Hand/Left Hand

The analogy I always use to describe this alliance between your talents and skills, and to stress the importance of knowing the difference, is universally understood. If you are innately right-handed, how often do you engage your left hand to write a note, unless there is a medical reason that has taken your right hand out of play? My guess is, never. And for all of you amazing lefties out there, please flip this analogy. I can already hear some of you playing devil's advocate, saying, "But if I practice really, really hard with my left hand, even if I am right-handed, my left-handed writing skills will eventually develop and improve." Yes, that's true. My response to you is, "Why would you want to set yourself up for that kind of struggle, when you could simply use the hand with which your writing *talent* supports the development of your writing *skill*?" What I want you to recognize is that having a job in which your talents support building the skills necessary for an exceptional performance in that role makes logical sense. It sets you up for performance success in a very practical way.

The benefit of using your talents to build your skills is that your end product will reach a higher level of excellence along a much faster trajectory than if you're not using your talents to drive your performance. And, I will add, it will never *feel as good*. Using the "wrong hand" to develop key skills necessary to successfully perform your job is absolutely not having the wind at your back. It's more like having a gale force wind hit you in the face each day as you struggle to perform your job. Believing in yourself absolutely includes the discovery and identification of your own unique talents. It's part of appreciating what sets you apart from others in the job market. It's also about recognizing what provides you with a competitive advantage in a right-fit job.

The Full Circle of Yourself

Warren Bennis was called the dean of leadership gurus by *Forbes* magazine and named one of the world's top ten thought leaders by *Businessweek*. He wrote more than twenty-seven books on business leadership, was nominated for a

Pulitzer Prize, and was an advisor to four US presidents. Dr. Bennis changed the face of business leadership beginning in the 1960s, forging new ground with regard to the need for leaders to possess and demonstrate authenticity, integrity, compassion, and inspiration through *collaboration*. Luckily for me, Dr. Bennis also spent the last thirty-five years of his career at USC's Marshall School of Business. He authentically walked the talk that he wrote about in his bestselling books. When I started to put together the first undergraduate career class I mentioned in my introduction, I came across a quote from Dr. Bennis about the role talent plays in a successful career. It's the quote I shared with you to open this chapter: "In a nutshell, the key to success is identifying those unique modules of talent within you and then finding the right arena to use them." He also said, "The model of progress is not linear; success is completing the full circle of yourself."

Both of these quotes are posted on my office wall as a source of inspiration in my own career. What I have discovered is that finding "unique modules of talent within you and then finding the right arena to use them" is exactly what your Functional Value point is all about. It's one of the reasons people who love their job, love their job. Connecting your talents and skills together in this close alliance, using your talents as a springboard for developing skills, will not only feel right and get you noticed at work, it will also play a key role in your own success story, as you learned from Thomas at the start of Step One. My own twist on what Dr. Bennis refers to as the "full circle of yourself" is the collective value of your three You Points, the "full" outside circle of the Working *You* system. This second You Point represents the exact reasons you have what it takes to succeed in a right-fit job and also why you should believe in yourself as a professional. Thank you, Dr. Bennis, for the inspiration.

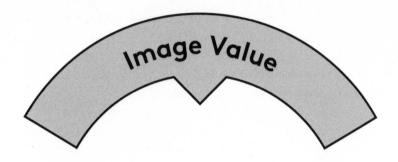

You Point #3: Your Image Value

This last You Point in the system is analogous to the proverbial cherry on top of a sundae. While it might not be the most significant ingredient of your three You Points, it's the ingredient that some might say makes your job taste the sweetest. Your Image Value is about two things: having your ego needs met and projecting a reputation to others that works in tandem with these needs to generate self-esteem. We will get into exactly what this means shortly, but don't confuse ego with obnoxious behavior. In this case, it is about meeting a human need to feel good about yourself and have an overall sense of pride about your job. Connecting your Image Value to the External Identity of what you do is what creates the final sparks to ignite the positive force that actually produces intrinsic motivation in the core center circle of the Working *You* system.

Your Image Value is ultimately defined by answering the following question: What job would make you proud to tell people what you do and where you do it? This third You Point is about being recognized by yourself and others as the *you* that you want to be in the world—and realizing how your job contributes to forming that important image.

One day I was reviewing material for a communication class I was teaching when Michael Tong, a senior majoring in public policy and business, came by to talk about an offer he had received to work for Teach for America after graduation. Michael felt pressure to make as much money as possible to pay off his student loans—and recognized that Teach for America certainly didn't offer that paycheck. Nevertheless, he felt strongly that the Teach for America job represented who he wanted to be in the world. Though Michael could certainly pursue a job in the private sector after he had fulfilled his two-year Teach for America contract, it was apparent that he was committed to figuring out how to balance his student loans with a teacher's salary so he could go down this path.

As a student, Michael had completed internships at PricewaterhouseCoopers in a consulting role and at Target, Inc., in the management training program. It was no surprise to me that, in addition to Teach for America, he received offers from both PricewaterhouseCoopers and Target. I remember thinking at the time how much I admired Michael for staying true to what he believes in and for prioritizing the importance of feeling good about what he contributes to the world through his work.

After Michael left my office and I continued to prepare for class, I pulled out Maslow's hierarchy of needs—likely the best-known theory of human motivation in existence (see diagram on page 28). A humanistic psychologist, Abraham Maslow believed that all of our actions are motivated by our drive to meet certain individual human needs. In this way, the Image Value point and Michael's need to feel good about who he is in the world of work came together in a powerful and rewarding way.

Your Image Value is defined through two key attributes, ego and reputation, so let's look at both.

Ego

If you look up the definition of *ego* in the dictionary, you'll find a lot of words preceded by the word *self*: self-importance, self-worth, self-respect, and self-esteem. But if you take a deeper dive into the definition of ego, you'll also discover that ego is very much about dignity, achievement, and ultimately independence. It isn't about narcissism or being a jerk. For our purposes of finding a right fit, your ego is about what you need to feel good about who you are and, in a right fit, your job should contribute to all of those *self* words, including self-esteem.

Reputation

The classic definition of *reputation* centers on the beliefs or opinions that are held by others about someone or something. In the Working *You* system, "someone" is you and "something" is your job. You might be asking, "Does it really matter what other people think?" My answer is that it does matter. Think about how you feel when someone pats you on the back and says "good job," or offers similar positive accolades. This second attribute in your Image Value point isn't about letting others define you. Instead, it's about being recognized as the person you want to be in the world and it circles back to and supports the dignity, accomplishment, and independence associated with having your ego needs met. Your job *should* be about you, and I want you to feel good about owning that objective.

Maslow's Hierarchy of Needs

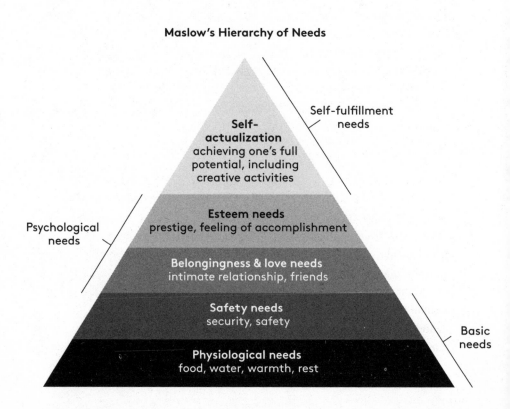

Human Needs

In Maslow's hierarchy of needs, he classifies human needs into five levels of a pyramid. The idea is to work from the bottom of the pyramid up, starting with our most basic physiological human needs (like food and water) and moving up through the levels until we reach self-actualization at the very top, or what I call in my career classes, "living your best life." To get to the top, we must pass through—and have our needs met—at each level, which includes the gateway to self-actualization, *esteem*. Maslow believed that esteem is ultimately about the belief in our own value as it relates to a feeling of accomplishment based on self-esteem, or *ego*, as we define it in this last You Point. Maslow also believed that esteem was based on the value we feel through the eyes of other people, or *reputation*. When both of these needs are met, one coming from an internal source (ego) and one from an external source (reputation), we can then move on to the final rung of self-actualization and living our best life.

When people do not have their esteem needs met, they often don't think of themselves as being *worthy* of living their best life. Therefore, they are less persistent about achieving their goals because they are less motivated to do so. This is a dynamic similar to the one I see again and again when students pursue jobs that won't make them proud to tell people what they do and where they do it. Why? Because their ego and reputation needs are not being met. In other words, the way we want the world to see us and the way in which the world *actually* sees us need to be in harmony. There's absolutely a connection between these two parts of your Image Value point. The internally sourced *ego* and externally sourced *reputation* align and work together in a right fit to support and project the image of who we want to be in the world. This relationship can be either positive or negative. In Michael's case, it was a positive relationship. Through his experience at Teach for America, he gained some insightful knowledge that he'll share with you at the end of this chapter.

Remember, your Image Value isn't narcissistic or bad. It represents real human needs and plays an important role in a right-fit job. Recognize it, define it, and give it value. It matters more to finding your own right path than you may have considered.

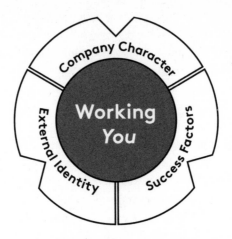

The Employer Points

Now that you are an expert on why you have value in the world of work, let's take a look at how your three Value Points correlate with the Employer Points: the Company Character, the Success Factors, and the External Identity. In Step Two of this book, I'll go into greater detail about each of the Employer Points as I help you identify fields, employers, and roles that represent your right-fit jobs. But for now, the most important thing is simply to understand what each Employer Point represents in the Working *You* system.

The Company Character

The first Employer Point correlates with Your Human Value and reflects the degree to which the employer's environment or *character* welcomes and respects someone like *you* as reflected through your demographics, personality, and motivational work triggers. The Company Character is about the detectable expression of the nature or features of the company that distinguish its overall environment. An example of getting a tree-top look at a company's character would be to look at leadership positions within the organization and ask yourself, "Are people with attributes of Human Value similar to mine being rewarded in that environment?" It's also important to examine the advancement pipeline. Who is moving up? Do you see others who you believe share similar demographics being recognized as valuable because they are advancing? Later, when you identify specific right-fit employers, I will help you dig deeper to find out what your target employers are all about from the inside out, in order to determine whether these are places that will indeed have your back at this most personal level.

The Success Factors

The second Employer Point correlates to Your Functional Value and reflects the degree to which your talents and skills support a successful job performance. The Success Factors are the functional conditions behind the job that will either set you up to experience the wind at your back or, conversely, be the gale force wind in your face as you strive to successfully perform your job. For example, looking at the talents and skills of people who are getting excellent performance reviews in the roles you are interested in, or who have recently been promoted out of the kinds of roles you are targeting, is just one way to determine the Success Factors of any particular role. Your goal, when we get there later in the book, will be to determine whether your own innate and developed abilities will support similar positive outcomes. Ask yourself, "Do I have the performance abilities (ideally fueled by my talents) to meet and go beyond the job's basic functional requirements?" Your answer will provide you with specific information you can use to make sure this second fit point in the system is connected and locked into place.

The External Identity

The third Employer Point correlates to Your Image Value and reflects the degree to which your ego and reputation needs are met by how the field, company, and role are viewed by you and others in a positive way. Is there a match between what *you* need to be proud to tell people what you do and where you do it? Ask yourself, "Does this job support the image I want to project to the world?" Your answer will provide you with the insight necessary to lock in this final connection point to ignite the force you need to be Working *You*. We will explore several ways to determine the External Identity of a potential employer. Living in the age of connection and transparency makes locking in this final fit point between you and your job straightforward and stress-free.

When You Care, It's Worth It

The following advice from Michael Tong perfectly embodies the note of promise on which I want to end this chapter. Remember, you *can* find your own right fit and be successful, because you have unique value. Trust in your distinctive and exclusive light, and it will take you to amazing places.

"My first year of teaching was the hardest ever, because I kept asking myself, 'Are the kids learning?' Because I was struggling to live on a teacher's salary, the other question I kept asking was, 'Did I make the right decision?' Then the teaching results came in, and all of the reasons why I went to work for Teach for America really rang true. *I was making a difference in a way that mattered to me.*

"I would be lying if I said it wasn't a really hard decision not to go for the money instead of sticking to what I really wanted to do and who I really wanted to be. Teaching honestly feeds my ego to the nth degree. But it was a really soul-searching decision. My family worked hard to send me to college, and here I was taking a job that paid a lot less than my other offers. But then a lot of good things happened really quickly. First came the good learning results from my students. Then I was offered a job as an assistant principal at the school I moved to the second year. I thought about it but didn't take it, because the money wasn't substantially different and the administrative part of the job wasn't exactly what I wanted to do.

"I was also offered a position by Teach for America to become the recruitment manager for Stanford. But then the best offer came through, and I really believe it's because I was true to myself in the first place, which put me in the *right place*. The school I was assigned to work at as a first-year teacher offered me an opportunity to be the director of data analytics. It was a new role that combines education and business, and the salary was what I needed to live a good life. I really never thought I would be here this fast. I may decide to get my MBA as a tool to do more good in the world in a way that matters to me, and I will explore that road at the right time. What I can tell you is all the reasons that drove me to make that hard decision to go into teaching and be true to myself are continuing to be validated and rewarded."

Check In . . .

My hope is that you are now beginning to see just how important you are in the quest to find your perfect job. A right-fit job requires *you*, first and foremost. We have already covered all of the basics of the Working *You* system, and now it's time to begin personalizing each step in a way that will make a difference uniquely for you. Finding work you love, like most valuable commodities in life, doesn't just happen. It takes engagement and believing that you are worth the investment. The timeline for making this happen depends on where you are right now, whether a freshman, sophomore, junior, senior, or already graduated. The common thread for each timeline is that you are worth your time. So let's spend some more time on *you*.

2

Defining Your Human Value

"The unique must be fulfilled."
—Martha Graham

Although the word *influencer* has taken on new meaning in the world driven by social media, influencers have always existed. Companies and organizations, cultural movements, movies, music, television shows—and the people connected to them—have always had the potential to become influencers.

For example, in the 1970s the late-night comedy show *Saturday Night Live* was an influencer. It's doubtful that anyone watching the show back then would have predicted it would still be an influencer all these decades later. Comedian Gilda Radner, an influencer and member of the original cast, offered the following words as she engaged in a fight against the cancer that would ultimately take her life at just forty-two years of age: "While we have the gift of life, it seems to me the only tragedy is to allow part of us to die—whether it is our spirit, our creativity or our glorious uniqueness." Her timeless advice is particularly relevant to the goal of this chapter.

I want you to start thinking about your Human Value as the cornerstone of your own "glorious uniqueness" and to realize that you have the potential to become an influencer when your uniqueness is rewarded in a right-fit job. Dancer Martha Graham, whose quote opens this chapter, gave similar advice when she said "the unique must be fulfilled." I chose this quote from Graham because she walked the talk of these words in her very long and successful life. Born at a time when people didn't plan their careers in the same way that we do today, Graham understood the importance of recognizing what makes one unique and then leveraging that to fulfill one's potential. Hers was a strategy that definitely paid off. Known as the woman who forever changed dance, Graham is often referred to as being to dance what Pablo Picasso was to art and Frank Lloyd Wright was to architecture. At age eighty-two, she was awarded the Presidential Medal of Freedom, the highest civilian honor given in the United States, and she continued to choreograph until her death at ninety-six. As you begin to discover and identify your collective value, including this first most important Human Value point, consider that fulfilling one's uniqueness is what makes influencers *influential*. And it's what will make you an influencer too.

As I explained in chapter 1, your Human Value is made up of three primary attributes:

#1: Your Demographics

#2: Your Personality

#3: Your Motivational Work Triggers

As you move forward, you will discover why having a job in which you are rewarded and not punished for who you are in the world of work begins with this first most personal You Point of Human Value. By the end of this chapter, you will have identified what this uniquely represents for you.

#1: The Value of Your Demographics

The Deloitte University Leadership Center for Inclusion found that across more than three thousand employees of different ages, religious beliefs, genders, ethnicities, sexual orientations, educational backgrounds, and physical abilities, more than 61 percent reported that they are not able to be who they are at work at this most fundamental demographic level. That means that basically six out of ten people surveyed don't feel appreciated for their *human value* at work, and as a result their sense of self was significantly undermined. It's no surprise that these same employees also felt forced to deny or hide who they are because they believed their employers demanded it. This is definitely an example of what it means to work against yourself.

If you don't identify with what traditionally might be categorized as an underrepresented group, you might think this first ingredient doesn't apply to you. If so, consider that within this same group of employees, 45 percent of straight white males also reported hiding personal demographic descriptors ranging from age to family background to cognitive and physical realities because they believed these factors would work against them.

Here's why it matters that you get this first part of your Human Value point locked into place with the Company Character of an employer. Research proves that employees who are less stressed about feeling they have to hide some part of who they are at work are also much more likely to be content, effective, and powerful in their jobs. When you're valued for *you* at this fundamental level, the likelihood that you will bring a higher degree of engagement, creativity, and commitment to excellence to your job is significantly increased. On top of that, the effectiveness of your interpersonal workplace relationships, which play a key role in your development and progression, is significantly enhanced when you are free to be yourself at work. It's difficult to effectively and authentically communicate and connect with other people when you're not *working you*.

Working *You*: Identifying Your Demographics

Write down all of the descriptors that define your demographics, including age, gender identification, education level, cultural background, sexual orientation, cognitive and physical realities, and even marital status if it applies (see the sample templates shown for Cara and Sam on pages 39 and 40 as examples). Think of this practice as taking your own census—cataloging the most foundational demographic descriptors of your Human Value in this first You Point. In defining these descriptors, you are identifying important criteria that you will use later to lead you to a right fit. Remember, whatever these descriptors may be for you, they will have value for the right employer. Follow Cara and Sam's lead and you won't get lost. *Who you are is all you need to know.*

Difference as a Strength

Brian graduated with a degree in social ecology from a state university in the Midwest. As a new college student, he had been diagnosed with ADHD after struggling to focus in his classes and complete assignments. When I interviewed him, we initially didn't zero in on this facet of his demographics because I didn't know about it. As we began to talk about his current job in real estate and why he loves doing what he's doing, he shared the following experience, which emphasizes the importance of recognizing that who you are as a human being at a fundamental level has value in the world of work—even if the world may not always see that value.

Brian told me, "I had challenges in junior high and high school, but it never became the barrier it was in college, when things suddenly became a lot harder, with tighter deadlines. I worried a lot about finding and keeping a job after I graduated, because after I was diagnosed a friend's mom told me that people with ADHD earn less money than other people. Nice, right? But then one of my advisors at college told me about David Neeleman."

David Neeleman, the founder of JetBlue, is very open about his ADHD; he believes it has professional value relative to his own career path. In *ADDitude Magazine*, Neeleman said, "My ADHD brain naturally searches for better ways of doing things." Neeleman has spoken in interviews about being able to quickly understand complex ideas and facts in order to come up with viable and simple solutions to problems. Brian, however, had the opposite experience in an internship he did between his junior and senior years of college, where he felt "confined and restricted"; it was "definitely not a right fit."

About that experience, he said, "I had to work with my computer a lot and do a ton of spreadsheets. I hated it and had a hard time seeing how I was ever going to hold a job or be successful. I kept thinking back to what my friend's mom had told me, which sometimes played like a bad sound loop in my head whenever I was down. But I read as much as I could about David Neeleman and found a lot of other really successful people who have ADHD."

Then the tide started to turn for him. "I love real estate, and it's always been an interest. I love all of the TV shows where people take run-down old houses and turn them around for profit." He laughed. "I'm that guy who watches all the real estate flipping shows. I started to see how what they were doing in these shows was something I knew I could do and that my ADHD could actually work in my favor, because you have to go from project to project and problem to problem. It was the exact opposite of my internship that I hated and didn't do well at because I was expected to do the same thing over and over. That's just not me, and I finally started to realize that's okay."

The happy ending to this story is that Brian is now working for a midsize real estate development firm that requires him to go out and evaluate sites and properties for new projects as well as revitalization. He's also responsible for figuring out how to make that development happen on both the financial and construction sides. "I really believe my ADHD is working for me now like it works for David Neeleman. When other people are tired and have to stop, I just keep going. This job fits."

Demographics Template: Cara

Gender: Female

Age: 20

Cultural Identification:
Biracial

Socio-Economic Background:
Middle-class urban, Midwest
background/Chicago

Religious Affiliation:
Nonreligious

Sexual Orientation: Straight

Relationship Status: Single

College Standing:
First-semester sophomore
in college

Education: Pursuing BA
degree in economics with
minor in classical culture and
society, Haverford College,
Pennsylvania

Demographics Template: Sam

Gender: Male

Age: 22

Cultural Identification: Caucasian

Socio-Economic Background: Working-class background, West Coast/Southern California

Religious Affiliation: Spiritual

Sexual Orientation: Questioning

Relationship Status: Single

College Standing: First-semester senior in college

Education: Pursuing BS degree in natural sciences, San Diego State University, California

#2: The Value of Your Personality

Jobs have personalities just like people have personalities. So many new graduates are struggling in a job simply because their personality isn't a fit with the personality of the job. When this happens, it's both physically and emotionally draining. And if you're working against yourself all day, you may also end up feeling really bad about yourself. (Personality as I'm addressing it within this system has nothing to do with popularity. I think this is a common misperception and is why I've seen many students try to rig personality tests and assessments.) Later in this chapter, as part of identifying the value of your personality, I recommend that you take the Myers-Briggs Type Indicator personality assessment, which will increase your awareness of this second part of your Human Value within the system. Of course, no test or assessment can tell you exactly who you are—that final determination is up to you. But they do provide key insights you can use to help you better understand and appreciate the value of your own personality.

Introverts, Extroverts, and the Importance of Authenticity

Susan Cain, author of the *New York Times* bestselling book *Quiet: The Power of Introverts in a World That Can't Stop Talking*, tells people she dreams big and has audacious goals, and sees no contradiction between her high aspirations and her introverted personality. In her top-ranked TED Talk, which has more than twenty-five million views and counting, she shares how society often holds up the outgoing personality as the preferred behavior. She talks about how she bought into the belief that being bold and assertive was how she should behave, even though this behavior is not aligned with her authentic personality type. Cain says that buying into this belief actually led her to become a Wall Street lawyer rather than the writer she believes she was meant to be. She shares in her work that many introverts make this same mistake, discounting the value of their authentic personality to make "self-negating" choices to please others and conform to who they believe society wants them to be. Doing so, she warns, results in a loss to you, your colleagues, your communities, and ultimately a loss to the world. It's exactly the opposite of what Martha Graham advised when she talked about fulfilling your uniqueness.

Author J. K. Rowling often cites her introverted personality as being partly responsible for the creation of her iconic Harry Potter series. Rowling has stated in interviews that when she got the idea for Harry Potter, she didn't have a pen and was too shy to ask someone to borrow one. She sat on the train, and instead of writing she started to imagine the rich details surrounding her idea—one that ultimately made her a billionaire.

If you're still thinking that being an introvert might prevent you from being a successful leader, look no further than the former dean of the Harvard Law School, Martha Minow—or as Susan Cain calls her, "the ultimate quiet leader." Employed from 2009 to 2017 in one of the most prestigious and powerful roles in higher education, Minow also received Harvard's highest honor when she was appointed the 300th Anniversary University Professor. How influential is she? Barack Obama credits her as one of his life-changing teachers.

I'm Not Unfriendly

A recent graduate I interviewed brought to life the downside of playing against type. When we spoke, Sara had been out of college for less than a year, having earned a degree in art history from a small liberal arts college on the East Coast.

Between her junior and senior years, Sara interned for the summer at a museum in her hometown and loved it. She worked directly with the museum's conservation team, which meant interacting with experts who restore and preserve artifacts and paintings. When I asked her about this positive internship experience, she showed no lack of enthusiasm. When we peeled back the layers about why she loved it, I learned that for the most part, her work had been independently driven. Of course, she had supervisors, but cataloging, researching, and keeping track of the progress being made on each piece was something she did on her own. When I asked how much of her work was completed independently, she said, "It was roughly 75 percent just me, and 25 percent engaging with other people. It really was the perfect job, but when I graduated there wasn't an opportunity to join full-time due to budget constraints, so I began to look other places."

Making the conscious decision to stay in the art field, Sara took a job she saw listed on a job site as an assistant director at a gallery. It was primarily a sales position, which required her to be on the floor most of the day as well as to attend openings in the evenings. When I asked her to contrast this experience with her positive internship experience, she was clear and concise: "I grew to hate it really fast. The worst was that I started to feel like it was me. The second week I was there, I felt like something was wrong with me.

"I don't like being on all the time, and I do my best work on my own. I'm very self-driven. I usually avoid saying this because I worry that people will think it means I'm unfriendly. *I'm not unfriendly.* I have great relationships with my boyfriend, friends, and family, but people who don't know me might think I'm unfriendly because I just prefer to go about my life in a more independent way. When my gallery director started telling me to talk and smile more, it just felt so phony."

After a few months Sara was fired from the gallery after the director told her that she is cold and impersonal. "I cried all the way home—and for days after. It hurt. A lot." I'm pleased to report that Sara found her way to her own right path because she did something very smart. She reconnected with her boss from her very successful museum internship, who recommended her to a colleague at another museum. It turns out there was an available position at the other museum—a position that was never listed on a job site—and Sara got it.

In reference to her short-lived gallery job, Sara said, "I'll never do that again. If I hadn't had the support of my friends and family, I don't know if I would have been able to crawl out of that hole. I was lucky. A lot of my friends aren't so lucky. They are feeling really worried about their future, and it's because they are working in the wrong environment."

Understanding why something *does not* work is sometimes more valuable than understanding why it does. The key takeaway for you here is that no personality type is more or less valuable than any other, and as you will see, being an extrovert or an introvert is just one of the many facets of your personality. The most important thing to remember is that *all types are valuable.*

Personality Tests and Assessments

I want to say a few more words about the benefit of taking a personality test or assessment. It can be a very useful tool to increase self-awareness and personal insight. What I recommend to achieve your goal of fully identifying this part of your Human Value point is to take the Myers-Briggs Type Indicator (MBTI) assessment through your college's career center and have a career advisor or counselor walk you through the results. If your career center doesn't offer the MBTI, it is available for a fee from the official Myers & Briggs Foundation at MBTIonline.com. If you choose to work more independently, do an online search for other personality tests or assessments you feel might be best for you.

The reason I like the MBTI is that it centers around cognitive preferences that govern our energy and focus—and success in any job certainly requires both our energy and focus. For example, the MBTI results consist of four letters, each representing a preference for a cognitive function that potentially has a direct connection with what your employer may ask you to do in any specific role. I have put together a guide below to further explain your MBTI code as it specifically relates to your own individual Working You system. Use this as a supplement to the interpretation of the assessment you will receive from the experts at your college career center or from the official Myers & Briggs Foundation site. In the meantime, after the guide, go ahead and complete the first part of identifying the value of your personality (following the examples of Cara and Sam on pages 48 and 49), and then you can loop back later to fill in your own MBTI code or results from another personality test or assessment.

The MBTI and Working *You*

This brief guide is my own narrative and gives you an opportunity to better understand the role the MBTI plays relative to your personality in the Human Value point. What I want you to keep foremost in your mind is that all personality types are equally valuable, and the goal is simply to increase your self-awareness around the value of your own unique personality type.

Extroversion (E) or Introversion (I)
This first letter in your MBTI code isn't about who is the loudest or the quietest. Nor is it a measurement of one's popularity. And just so you don't waste time thinking you should be one or the other, there is no data supporting the idea that extroverts are more successful than introverts or vice versa. For our purposes, this first letter is about your energy source. Extroverts prefer to get their energy by engaging with the external world, whereas introverts prefer to gas up their tank by engaging in independent activities. For example, if you are an introvert and your job requires you to constantly engage with clients, make sales calls, attend events, and spend the majority of your time working in a team setting, you are going to be exhausted by noon. You want your preferred energy source and your job to be compatible. If you take the MBTI at your college's career center, I'm sure your advisor or counselor would agree that your preference doesn't mean you can't do the opposing dichotomy in any of the four areas represented in the assessment. It simply means that you have a preference. But for our purposes, preferences matter—because we are casting your preference as having value. Each of these will later factor into how you assess potential right fits.

Sensing (S) or Intuition (I)

This second letter in your MBTI code is about your preference for giving meaning to information based on fundamental facts (sensing) or based on a sixth sense or gut-level instinct (intuition). Because this letter focuses on how you take information in, it can be considered a cognitive function related to one's individual perception of what is meaningful. People with a preference for sensing often need to touch, see, and feel meaning based on their objective senses. A preference for intuition on the other hand means that even though objective facts are presented to you, you subjectively add another layer that produces meaning for you. A job that requires complete objectivity, for example, a science-oriented role in the medical or accounting fields, could be a better fit for someone with a sensing preference. However, if you prefer to give information meaning based on intuition, ask yourself if the job you are considering is going to play to type or work against it? For example, while a venture capitalist certainly has to pay attention to objective facts, someone in this position also relies heavily on gut-level meaning. This is an important function of your personality type that can greatly assist you when you look at a potential right fit.

Thinking (T) or Feeling (F)

Once you take information in and give it meaning, you often have to make decisions. This third cognitive function is very different from the previous one, because it requires you to act. People with a thinking preference utilize objective rationale to make decisions and are often described as "more head than heart." A preference for thinking can also be described as "logical" and "truth-focused." On the opposite side of this dichotomy is a preference for feeling, which means that you rely more on subjective rationale, including emotion and empathy as well as principles and values, to make decisions. For example, someone with a preference for thinking would be playing to type as a loan officer at a bank, whereas someone who might be swayed to make a loan based on emotion or empathy would be playing against type. A much better fit for someone with a feeling preference would be a customer service–based job like a teacher or a consultant. Consider the criteria for how the decision-making process is successfully played out in any role you are considering and how your preference for this particular cognitive function can possibly work for you or against you in a potential fit.

Judging (J) or Perceiving (P)

The last letter in your MBTI code deals with structure and how you engage with the outside world. It is not about being judgmental or how you view others or even yourself. People with a preference for judging typically live their lives in a more structured way than people with a preference for perceiving. If you have a judging preference, you may have a color-coded closet or a strictly scheduled itinerary for vacations: for example, at 9 a.m. meet in the hotel lobby; at 9:30 depart for the museum; at 11:30 reconvene in the museum's center hall for lunch. For someone with a perceiving preference, this kind of itinerary may sound like a vacation from hell. People with a perceiving preference typically prefer to keep things open and free-flowing. Their closets are likely not color-coded and, in fact, may be a bit messy. Those with a judging preference may view perceivers as procrastinating or disorganized. Likewise, people with a perceiving preference may view those with a judging preference as too inflexible. You can see how different jobs may play to or against your preference for structure. Relative to this last letter, considering how deadlines, scheduling, and even expectations about flexibility might play out in any potential role can significantly contribute to whether you will be going with the flow or swimming against the tide at work.

Percentages Matter

Pay attention to percentages! If you are close to the middle on any of these four dichotomies, you are more likely to be comfortable with either cognitive preference. If your scores are heavily weighted, what I would target as 20 to 25 percent either way, it indicates that you have a clear preference for that particular cognitive function, which could make a big difference in any given environment.

Working *You*: Identifying Your Personality

Write down your answers to the following two questions that often get asked in job interviews. These are actually critical to giving you information about your personality that you can use to find a right fit beyond a test or assessment. Feel completely free to answer honestly and candidly because these are only for you—and not for an interviewer. Answer the questions with a handful of adjectives or short phrases. As you answer the first question, remember that your answers have value, because all personality types are valuable. For the second question, think about asking for input from friends, family members, coworkers, supervisors, professors, or spiritual or religious advisors you trust to be both honest and constructive in their descriptions.

Question #1: How do you describe yourself?

Question #2: How do others describe you?

In Cara and Sam's examples (pages 48 and 49), these two questions are answered first in their templates. This is the subjective part of identifying your personality, while your MBTI code or results from another assessment provide an additional layer of objectivity. By defining and appreciating the value of your personality, you give yourself the information and criteria you need to connect who you are with the job. When you recognize this value, you will be better equipped to find a right fit, one where your personality and the personality of the job can work in harmony to achieve your goals.

Personality Template: Cara

How I Describe Myself

Outgoing. Optimistic. Inclusive. Visual. Competitive. Logical problem solver. Friendly, but you need to prove yourself to me. Good communicator. Limited patience. Watchful and wise. All in when motivated. Good sense of humor.

How Others Describe Me

Tough but fair. Fun. Likes attention. Smart and watchful. Calculated risk taker. Always rises to the occasion. Unafraid. Sometimes inappropriate.

MBTI (ESTJ)

- Extroverted (21%)
- Sensing (5%)
- Thinking (15%)
- Judging (20%)

MBTI Summary Points

I prefer to be with other people, but I can also do well when I have to work on my own. But I definitely wouldn't do well with a job where I am by myself all day long. I need other people to bounce ideas off of, and I want to see the reaction others have to my work and what I have to say. I am not afraid of some competition, and I like to lead and win. I definitely need you to prove your point, and I don't like to have my time wasted. I want to feel enough freedom to be creative and go my own way. Being boxed in by a job that doesn't require a certain level of autonomy sounds limiting. Actually, it sounds like prison.

Personality Template: Sam

How I Describe Myself

Smart. Fair. Insightful. Follows things through. Big-picture thinker. Practical dreamer. Goal-driven. Clear communicator. Results focused. Leader. Open-minded. Can be critical. Daring. Can be fearless.

How Others Describe Me

Independent. Decisive. Likes to be right. Holds himself to very high standards. Clear. Entrepreneurial. Out-of-the-box thinker. Brave. Confident. Nonconformist.

MBTI (INTP)

- Introverted (15%)
- Intuitive (20%)
- Thinking (25%)
- Perceiving (10%)

MBTI Summary Points

I don't like to be told what to do and prefer to work on my own. However, I do like to persuade others to follow me. I am good at making strategic decisions personally and professionally. Black-and-white scenarios don't work well for me, and I am good at finding new ways to solve problems. I can be impatient with others, but I am also impatient with myself. My instincts typically serve me well, and it takes time to gain my trust. I work hard and will put in whatever it takes to achieve my goals. I am definitely a perfectionist, and I expect a lot of myself. I also expect a lot from others. I'm me; take me or leave me, but don't ignore me.

#3: The Value of Your Motivational Work Triggers

Of course, work is about money. It's also about meaning. Can money have meaning? Definitely, but it only matters if it has meaning to you. Your motivational work triggers are core principles that can positively or negatively drive behavior that's engaged or disengaged in any given job. These triggers include both tangibles and intangibles. Tangible triggers are represented by things we can effectively touch and see, like money and job titles. Examples of intangible triggers are more ideals based, and might include working for a company devoted to diversity and inclusion, ethics, transparency, or even putting employees over profits. Again, whether tangible or intangible, it's all about what you define as meaningful.

Thinking about what motivates you at work in this context is important because everyone has different motivational triggers. And it's exactly for this reason that they are placed in this first You Point of Human Value: because they reflect who you are at a level that goes beyond your demographics and personality in order to drive behavior. I have found that motivational work triggers speak directly to what you need your job to give you in order to remain motivated into action at a fundamental and personal level. It's something I studied in my doctoral program at length and something I believe people often feel they can force themselves into feeling even if it isn't authentically there. In truth, it's not possible to force or fake this type of motivation in any sustainable fashion. The best way I can describe this is to say that when your authentic motivational work triggers are met by your employer, you get what I call a *soul reward*.

Soul Reward

Erin Curry received a bachelor of fine arts degree in fiber design from the SUNY College at Buffalo and an associate in applied science degree in textile and surface design from the Fashion Institute of Technology. Her first job out of college was for a custom trade–only carpet showroom in Manhattan, where she joined as an artist and then moved on to a more administrative role as the executive assistant to the president of sales. From there, she progressed to two other roles with design firms centered around e-commerce and marketing before assuming her current role as the content marketing manager for St. Frank. St. Frank is a successful textile and home goods company with the mission of providing customers with beautiful and authentic home luxuries through partnerships with artisans from around the world. Core to St. Frank is its twofold social mission to support economic empowerment for artisans and preserve traditional artisanal crafts.

In her current role, Erin is not only connected to the mission of her employer, she is also clearly bringing her design education into play. Being motivated by what her employer is trying to achieve in the world and what it represents has everything to do with what motivates Erin personally. One part of St. Frank's mission that resonated for her was that the artisans who create these products are from low- and middle-income countries. The company works with artisan organizations that follow fair trade principles with a mission of preserving culturally significant crafts and fairly compensating the artists who make them.

"Ethical values are important for me to feel motivated by the work. Not only in terms of brand practices, but also with the interpersonal practices of the company's leaders. I think fairness and rationality are important aspects of a healthy work environment, and having leaders who are able to build a layer of trust with their employees makes a huge difference for me. At St. Frank, we have a small team that works together really closely, regardless of the geographical distance between locations. We travel together and often spend time together outside of work. All of these things are important to me, and it wouldn't be possible without trust. Trust is right up there for me when it comes to what I need personally to be all in. I also need to feel a connection between where I want to go in the future and what I do every day. I didn't even know this was part of the company's culture before I interviewed, but they made sure that my path within the company and my own career path were aligned. For me, it's one of the reasons why the trust is there."

Working *You*: Identifying Your Motivational Work Triggers

Make a comprehensive and thoughtful list that represents both the tangible and intangible triggers that will motivate you to positively drive engagement; make them real by writing about why they are important to you. No, it's not enough to just think about them. When you write them down, they crystallize and become real. And that *realness* is what you will use later to identify your right fit.

Remember, tangible triggers are about what the job gives you in the form of something you can effectively touch or see—for example, money, job titles, job security, work/life balance, opportunities for promotion, and so on. Intangible triggers are about your personal and professional ideals—for example, integrity, ethics, transparency, trust, providing service to others, and so on. Before you make your list, take a look at how Cara and Sam identified their motivational work triggers, and then follow suit. I suggest you spend some quality time thinking and writing about what inspires you and creates meaning, because connecting your motivational work triggers in a right fit makes a big contribution to a happy and sustainable successful outcome.

Motivational Work Triggers Template: Cara

Tangible Triggers

Equitable pay. Clear advancement criteria. Respected job title. Good health benefits. A 401K plan and/or stock options. Attractive office setting. Flexible scheduling. Paid vacation days.

Intangible Triggers

Inclusive workplaces. Diversity. Open-door communication. People and profits, not just profits. Tasks that require teamwork. An environment that is social. High-energy colleagues.

Summary Points

I need a diverse group of people to work with, but to stay motivated, it also has to be inclusive. It's the kind of leadership I need, and the kind of leader I want to be. Working only with people who are like me would be boring. I am motivated by fairness, and that means being paid a salary that reflects my contributions. In addition, I want good benefits that will give me the security I need to handle life on my own after college. I am also motivated if there is flexibility that allows me to work at home or remotely sometimes. The aesthetic value of my surroundings will motivate me; a visually unappealing building or office will not. I am definitely motivated by what I see.

Motivational Work Triggers Template: Sam

Tangible Triggers

Open-ended promotional opportunities. Salary based on performance, not pay grade ranges. Flexible hours. Clear rubrics for performance evaluation.

Intangible Triggers

Nonjudgmental environments and people. Leaders who listen and take risks. Meritocratic environment. Intellectual stimulation. Unilateral communication—not limited by hierarchy. Goal-driven people and leaders.

Summary Points

I am motivated by opportunities that are not limited by set-in-stone expectations. Doing something just because it has always been done that way is demotivating. I want to work independently more than in teams but be able to talk to everyone in the company if I have an idea or need feedback. I am motivated by the opportunity to grow and get paid at a rate that reflects my abilities and contributions. Being limited by preset pay ranges is not inspiring to me. I need to be in an environment where people can be themselves and express who they are in a positive way. I want some control over my time and where and when I will do my best work. Punching a time clock or being judged by the number of hours I spend at my desk sounds very confining. I really don't want to be in a job in which my every move is watched. Autonomy is motivational!

Check In . . .

Success that is sustaining as well as evolving will arguably always draw on the unique strength of your Human Value. Recognizing and using these very personal attributes of who you are will serve as the solid ground under your feet as you carry out your work. When your "glorious uniqueness" is recognized, leveraged, and rewarded by your employer, *you will be an influencer*. Don't allow these most personal attributes to be dimmed or covered up. Your human uniqueness, rooted in your demographics, personality, and motivational work triggers, will not only make you influential, but they are also the source of your other two You Points. They are *you*. They are *unique*. And as we move ahead, never forget "the unique must be fulfilled."

3

Defining Your Functional Value

"His talent was as natural as the pattern that was made by the dust on a butterfly's wings."
—Ernest Hemingway

The above quote is from the first part of a passage Ernest Hemingway wrote in his memoir, *A Moveable Feast*. The book chronicles his life as a struggling writer in 1920s Paris during what is often referred to as the Jazz Age, between World Wars I and II. Hemingway was talking about the acclaimed writer F. Scott Fitzgerald, whose masterpieces include *The Beautiful and Damned* and *The Great Gatsby*. In the next sentence of this passage he wrote, "At one time he understood it no more than the butterfly did and he did not know when it was brushed or marred." Hemingway claims that Fitzgerald lost the "effortless expression" of his talent because he didn't respect or nurture it.

This rather stark message about the need to respect and nurture your talent is extremely relevant to the main point of this chapter. Why? Because a right fit will allow you to effortlessly express your talent. To make that happen—not just in your first job, but throughout your career—I want you to recognize the importance of keeping your talents close by and in play. The truth is that if you do respect and nurture them, and you place yourself in roles that reward them, your talents will unlock the door to a lifetime of successful job performances. The alternative—ignoring, denying, or even destroying your talents—represents a loss not only for you, but also for everyone else. The world is a better place when everyone's individual talents are employed.

Your Functional Value is made up of two primary attributes:

#1: Your Talents

#2: Your Skills

But first, let's address the elephant that may have lumbered ever so quietly—or loudly—into the room. If you're thinking *I don't have talent*, let me reassure you: Yes, you do. In class, we often have an hour-long discussion about this, as I painstakingly prove to each and every student that they already possess the talent they need to succeed in a right fit. So let me just say, if you're breathing, you have talents. Stick with me on this, and at the end of the chapter, let's check back in to see if the elephant has left the room.

#1: The Value of Your Talents

Your Functional Value point is about creating collaboration between your talents and skills. As I mentioned earlier in the book, your talents should ideally serve as the wind at your back to support your job performance and act as the foundation for the developed abilities (skills) you list on your resume.

If you enter the word *talent* into Google, you'll see the following definitions:

general intelligence or mental power: ability

a special often athletic, creative, or artistic aptitude

Merriam-Webster adds an archaic definition:

a characteristic feature, aptitude, or disposition of a person

This one hits the sweet spot, getting to the heart of a deeper meaning of talent relative to setting yourself up for success at work. *Sooner or later, everything old is new again.*

While the first two definitions of talent aren't wrong, by folding in this third definition you gain the opportunity to uncover the full force of your talents as they uniquely relate to who you are in the world of work. The distinction is important because for those recent graduates who love their job and are already being promoted, their talents, cast primarily as *behavioral characteristic* and *special aptitudes* (as defined in the Working *You* system), are truly being leveraged to turn in a successful—not mediocre—job performance.

Below is a word cloud with examples of what talents, set within this expanded meaning of the word, represent in the Working *You* system. Of course, this doesn't even scratch the surface of all the talents that exist in the world, including yours. The goal is for you to simply begin to recognize how talents are defined here so you can start to not only discover and identify your own talents, but also employ them.

Sneakers and Talent and a Side Hustle

〜〜〜

Alex graduated from Bowling Green State University in Ohio with a bachelor of fine arts degree in graphic design. His career after college has had two simultaneous paths: working a full-time job while pursuing his own business. It's a career combination I see becoming more common for a lot of new college graduates. I'm sharing Alex's story within the context of talents because for those who are successfully managing these two paths, there is an overwhelming crossover of talent utilization. The key takeaway is if you're using your talents successfully during the day, and your own venture calls on the same talents, you're allowing both paths to work collaboratively. And if you hate your day job, it's absolutely going to drain the energy you need to pursue your entrepreneurial interests. Both paths should be leveraging your talents.

Alex works full-time for a graphic design company during the day, using his arts degree. When I asked him about the talents he brings to both paths, he listed the following: *creativity, storytelling, detail focused, listening to others*. As for his special aptitude talent for design, he describes it as his "realm of content." I like that description.

Alex shared with me, "When I'm able to continually engage with my talents as part of my work, the final product is always above and beyond what I produce if I'm not engaging my talents. I think one reason this is true is because I don't like doing something that *doesn't* require my talents. Putting my talents into action makes me feel a bit special."

Right now, Alex affectionately calls his entrepreneurial path his "side hustle," but he's actually building a name for himself customizing sneakers with his original designs. It's an emerging new field that blends original art and apparel. According to the *New York Times*, the demand for customization within the $29 billion sneakers market is growing and reflects society's increasing desire for customization in general. When I asked Alex why he started his own company in this new field, he said, "I love to play golf, and I'm also a big basketball fan. I also love sports shoes and sneakers, which is the core of my side hustle. I've always had a big collection of sneakers. As a designer, I view shoes as an opportunity for people to express themselves while doing what they love, like golf or basketball. It's an avenue most graphic designers don't explore, but it's totally right for me. I love working with a client, getting to know them, and coming up with a custom design that's perfect for them. That's where my talent for listening to others comes into play. It's the same thing I do with my full-time job as a graphic designer. In both roles, I tell stories with my designs. Sneakers are made of canvas, so instead of designing and painting on an art canvas, I design on sneakers. Because I'm good at it, I love it. I honestly don't know how you can love something if you aren't naturally good at it. To me, that's why we have talents, so we can put them to use."

Working *You*: Identifying Your Talents

When identifying this part of your Functional Value point, you may have to do some discovering, so consider the experience-based questions below as ways to help you recognize or uncover talents. Ask yourself, "What are those behavioral characteristics or possibly even special aptitudes that can connect who I am to what I do in a way that will drive a stellar job performance?" Everything certainly doesn't apply to everyone, which is exactly why your talents create an advantage distinctively for you. Talents, as you can hopefully now see, come in a wide variety of valuable flavors.

Because talents play such an important part in a right-fit job, I have put together a comprehensive approach in the coming pages to help you uncover your individual talents. Also, check out the completed templates from Cara and Sam at the end of this chapter to help you stay on track and see how all of these layers come together to create clarity for the talents you uniquely bring to the job market. Take your time; I don't want you to overlook these important building blocks for your Functional Value.

Computers and Talent and a Bad Fit

〰〰〰

Finding a job is without a doubt one of the most personal endeavors life asks us to do, because it means we have to put ourselves out there in a big way. It brings up a lot of doubts and fears as well as excitement and hope for the future. I was continually amazed by the willingness of the people I met while writing this book to share with such candor what were often very personal and challenging experiences. When I interviewed Sophia, we quickly began talking about talents and skills, and the fact that they are two different things but should ideally work together. Sophia had recently graduated with a degree in computer engineering from a private college in the South, and she described her top talents as *caring*, *curious*, *problem solving*, and *methodical*. She did well in college, and her talent for problem solving and being methodical served her well in her core coursework. "I love testing things. I'm good at finding problems and fixing them. One of my professors said I was the best debugger he had ever had as a student, and to me, that was like the best compliment he could give me."

After graduation, Sophia moved back to her hometown of Chicago and started looking for a job. "There's a really good alumni network in Chicago, and I had a lot of support from people letting me know about jobs. Lucky for me, computer engineering is one of those majors that's very much in demand right now. But still, I made a bad choice. A really bad choice."

What Sophia described is something that often happens. New graduates start their search by first looking at the job—and not at themselves. Externals tend to be evaluated with limited internal assessment. When I asked her more about why it was a bad choice, she shared, "At one point I had five callback interviews, and I honestly didn't look too hard at what each company was all about from the inside out. I was only looking at them from the outside in."

Of the three offers Sophia received, she chose the job that had the second highest salary and where the company was most often in the press. "It was a name brand, and that mattered to me. But that wasn't the problem. The problem was that the job only needed my left-side brain, and I actually have a pretty healthy right-side brain too."

The job, with a highly respected robotics company, required her to do a lot of independent work more focused on maintaining existing technologies than on breaking new ground. "I struggled in a lot of ways, because what I had to do most of the time didn't play to my strengths, which is how I now see it. I loved my algorithm classes in college, which to a degree is all about problem solving. In the job, I was unfortunately mostly running tests to make sure things were working right versus fixing things that were wrong and discovering new ways to innovate. Even when I did find a problem, it was farmed out to a different department. I really didn't get to interact with anyone very much except my immediate boss. I mean, there were other people in my department, but everyone sort of operated as their own island and no one seemed very happy. I'm really good with people, listening to what they need, caring about them, and figuring out how I can help them. But it didn't seem like this mattered at all. I was only asked to check systems to make sure they were running correctly, and I was definitely not supposed to have any interaction with our clients."

Over a period of six months, Sophia often received negative feedback from her boss and started to feel that she might be fired. "I was starting to get really depressed. Some days I came home and felt like the world's biggest loser. It was such a different feeling for me, because in college I never struggled beyond just meeting the deadlines of a heavy class load. Even then, I always turned in a good performance."

Her family, recognizing that she was becoming more and more unhappy, suggested she simply quit and look for another job that was a better fit. "There were lots of tears. They were more worried about my mental health than my career, and I actually went on medication. Finally, I did quit without having another job lined up, which I know isn't the smartest thing to do. One day on my way to work I had a panic attack, and that had never happened to me before. It was awful. And it scared me."

After leaving the job, Sophia was too embarrassed to go back to her alumni network to solicit their help. Instead, she reconnected with the recruiter from one of the other companies she had turned down months earlier to see if the offer was still a possibility. "For whatever reason, the recruiter was so nice to me when I called. We met for coffee and I told her what had happened. I wasn't planning to tell her, but it all just spilled out. I vowed not to list the robotics job on my resume, and it definitely isn't there. But she convinced me to use it as a learning experience and gave me a lot of support." Sophia was heartbroken when the recruiter then conveyed that the original job was no longer available. "My heart sank. I remember feeling like I was going to throw up, sitting across from her at the table." But the interview quickly turned hopeful when the recruiter told her that she knew of another company that was hiring and

continued

offered to connect her. "She saw something in me that I didn't see at the time. She knew me as a student coming out of college months before, and saw what went wrong. I'm so grateful she referred me to a job that she thought would fit. It did. She knew a lot more about me than I knew about myself, and I'll forever be grateful."

Sophia's first job was a bad fit because it didn't allow her to engage her talents beyond being methodical. The point to take away from her experience is that we have more than just one talent, and our top talents need to become that anchor that supports the performance people see above the waterline. Sophia's story ended well. She got the job at the company this angel of a recruiter connected her to, and the outcome has been radically different. When I asked her about her new job,

she said, "I'm back doing what I do best, debugging and solving problems. It's a lot smaller company, but it's growing, and that excites me too. I also get to be part of client meetings, which I love, love, love. My boss said I add a lot of value because the customers like me. I think sometimes my boss listens to me more than some of my colleagues because of my ability to connect with clients." Sophia's voice had so much more energy talking about her new job. "After a year," she excitedly told me, "I'm eligible for ownership options, which in the future could pay really big dividends if our company goes public." Then she added a final note about why this job is so different than the job she quit. "I never felt connected to my first job, like there should be somebody else doing it. In my new job, I feel like I'm the person who should be doing it."

Part A: What Are Your Top Talents?

Here are some questions to get you started in your own talent discovery:

1. What do you do when you lose all track of time successfully engaged in an activity? Maybe it's in a favorite class, maybe it's when engaging in a hobby. What talents are supporting these endeavors? Go back to the word cloud to revisit how we are defining talents and draw some lines of connection between what you would define as successful activities and the *talents* that support them. Definitely add any talents that you recognize in yourself that aren't on the word cloud.

2. What are you good at? Think of school or work assignments for which the professor or your boss has praised you for your work. Think about the context and conditions that are in play when you do your best work. What talents are supporting these successful deliverables?
3. What single act are you most proud of when you reflect on your life to date? Identify the talents that you believe supported you in that achievement.

Part B: Take a Talent Inventory

Here's another layer to add even more depth to the discovery of your talents. Take a *talent inventory* as you assess how you prefer to live your daily life. For example, let's say you make breakfast for yourself. Upon finishing, you immediately wash or rinse the dishes off before placing them in the dishwasher (if that's relevant to your kitchen). Then you move on to cleaning the table and countertop. You might choose the word *meticulous* as a talent. Or maybe in class you sat next to a student from a different country and you immediately began to ask them about their national culture because you are genuinely curious about the life experiences of others. In that case, write down the word *curious* as a talent. You can do this based on memory, or over the course of a day. Then reflect on your list at the end of the day, thinking about the talents that innately underwrote your preferred actions.

Part C: Influential Talents

Now, from all of the talents you just listed in A and B, which words or descriptions keep coming up again and again? Do any of your talents have a dotted line connection to your personality? For example, if your MBTI code includes an F for Feeling and you also list empathy as a talent, pay close attention to this connection because it spans two You Points. This is likely to be an *influential talent* for you. After you've made your list of influential talents, rank them into a top five list like Cara and Sam (pages 66–69).

Talents Template: Cara

Part A

When do I lose all track of time? Playing tennis. Hiking with friends. Working on a group project when I am the leader. Being at music festivals. Putting a speech together. Being the first in my group to solve a problem or solving a problem in general.

Supporting Talents: Bold. Competitive. Determined. Forceful. Outgoing. Social. Athletic. Agile. Rational/Logical. Detail-oriented. Astute.

What am I good at? Case Competitions. Public speaking. Quantitative questions/assignments. Delegating. Organizing and managing people. Prioritizing my time. Finding potential problems before they occur.

Supporting Talents: Tactical. Competitive. Outgoing. Communicator. Driven. Clever. Shrewd. Focused. Vigilant. Logical.

What three acts or achievements am I most proud of when I reflect on my life? Being on a champion tennis team in high school. Winning a student case competition and representing my college at a regional event. Finding the right doctor and treatment center for my grandmother with Alzheimer's disease.

Supporting Talents: Competitive. Tactical. Bold. Self-regulation/Self-control. Persistent. Gritty. Caring.

Part B

Talent Inventory Summary:

- I get up early and review my day. I don't want to be late or overlook something important. (Organized. Detail-oriented. Self-starter.)
- Get to class and engage with friends. (Outgoing. Friendly. Social.)
- I noticed that at the end of class, I always do the same thing—look at the syllabus plan for the next class and ask any questions about an assignment or expectation that is unclear to me or for which I need more details. (Detail-oriented. Bold. Logical.)
- I get so bored if the professor repeats things because someone doesn't get it. (Quick-minded.)
- When I walk into the food court, I look around to see who is working, because part of my decision about where to go is about who does the best job making my favorite food and also which lines are going to be the fastest. (Strategic. Tactical. Expeditious.)
- When I'm in a group of friends, they ask my opinion a lot and often want me to advise them on topics from dating to family issues to school problems. (Astute. Problem solver. Communicator.)
- At the end of the day I make a list of tomorrow's to-dos, knowing I will go over it again in the morning. Sometimes I will remember things and go back and add them to my list before lights-out—or I will turn the lights back on and add them if I think they're a priority. (Thorough. Organized. Driven. Systematic.)

Part C

My Top Five Influential Talents:

Detail-oriented. Competitive. Logical problem solver. Communicator. Bold.

Talents Template: Sam

Part A

When do I lose all track of time? Brainstorming new business ideas. Writing a business plan. Watching *Game of Thrones*. Playing chess. Researching stock picks. Having a good political argument with someone smart. Snowboarding.

Supporting Talents: Creative. Innovative. Strategic. Risk taker. Imaginative. Resourceful. Independent. Determined. Tenacious. Curious. Writing.

What am I good at? Writing business plans. Following through and being persistent. Understanding the big picture. Connecting seemingly disparate ideas. Standing up for myself and others. Generating ideas.

Supporting Talents: Big-picture thinker. Competitive. Creative. Inventive. Resourceful. Brave. Nonconformist. Determined.

What three acts or achievements am I most proud of when I reflect on my life? Helping my dad start his new food business. Being selected for an internship at a national political convention sponsored by the Washington Center. Being an officer for the Entrepreneur Society at SDSU.

Supporting Talents: Resourceful. Creative. Inspired. Goal driven. Adventurous. Writing.

Part B

Talent Inventory Summary:

- My mind usually starts to race from idea to idea while I'm getting ready in the morning. It's good brainstorming time. (Inspired. Multitasker. Creative. Dedicated.)
- I don't really focus too much on the outside world on my way to class. And when I'm getting ready, I don't really want the TV or music on, because they interrupt my brain flow. (Independent. Innovative. Imaginative.)

- I find that I don't dive too deep into the nuts and bolts of an assignment at first. I immediately start thinking about execution versus planning. I'm seeing how I can make this great. (Inspired. Big-picture thinker. Confident. Curious.)
- I noticed that when I'm hanging out with friends, it's usually just one friend or maybe two at the most. Beyond that I feel like there are too many people to have any kind of quality time, even if it's just having fun. (Curious. Motivated. Observant.)
- If someone has an idea or if the professor asks a question, I don't have a problem sharing my thoughts even if they aren't fully developed. I'm not that afraid of making a mistake or saying something other people haven't expressed. (Brave. Nonconformist.)
- When working in a group, I get frustrated when I feel we aren't staying on track. Chatter for the sake of chatter is a waste of time. I find that I have to be careful about expressing myself too much on this subject or other people in the group will think I'm a jerk. (Strategic. Determined. Independent. Dedicated.)
- At the end of the day I have a hard time going to sleep because my mind is still racing. I've noticed that it's sort of full circle for me, because that's how I start my day. I do get some good ideas right before going to sleep, though. But then I finally just shut it down, usually because I'm wiped out. (Creative. Energetic. Determined.)

Part C

My Top Five Influential Talents:
Creative. Inspired. Determined. Dedicated. Curious.

#2: The Value of Your Skills

Skills are provable—and to a great extent contribute to why you will or will not get a job interview. Ideally, skills say a lot about who you are and what you can bring to a job. For example, if your resume offers up a lot of analytical experience, the reader will likely assume you are an analytical person. If your resume describes how you have led teams to success, the reader will likely assume you are motivational and a good communicator. These assumptions may or may not be an accurate depiction of your authentic Functional Value as we are defining it in the Working *You* system.

Remember, your goal is to have your talents and skills work in collaboration, because when your skills are anchored at the deeper level of talents, your resume will accurately depict the authenticity of your Functional Value. It's common to tweak your resume for a specific job, but sometimes your resume can start to depict someone who isn't you. And that can lead you to a bad fit. This is exactly why it's critical to examine the skills presented on your resume and, if needed, recalibrate to begin leveraging your talents as you build your skills moving forward. When your talents and skills are supporting each other, then the assumptions employers make about you when they read your resume will be backed up by *you*.

Will you ever have to perform tasks in a right-fit job that don't fully leverage your talents? Of course you will; we all live in the real world. However, you want to maintain a 70:30 percent sweet spot where you are leveraging your talents at least 70 percent of the time to successfully perform the requirements of your job. At this level, I've found that your Functional Value point stays locked into the correlating Success Factors. (I'll revisit this formula when you begin assessing your best right fits later on.)

Working *You*: Identifying Your Skills

To determine if you have been using your talents as foundational support to develop your skills, your resume is the best place to go to see the abilities you can "prove" (skills) and to get a better understanding of how you have been leaning into or away from your talents. If you follow the three action items on the next page, you will have the necessary insight to determine whether or not you have been leveraging your talents to build skills.

1. Print out your resume and compare it to your list of influential talents. How are your talents supporting or not supporting the development of the skills highlighted in the bullet points of your resume? Is there a strong collaborative connection? For example, if analyzing data is listed as a skill on your resume and talents such as methodical, logical, and detail-oriented are not represented as influential or even on your greater list of talents, you may not be leveraging your talents to build skills.

2. Next to your bullet points, which typically summarize skills utilized for that job or task, write down the primary talents you believe support that particular experience. It doesn't matter whether or not these talents are *your* talents, because now you will determine if you have been leaning into or away from your own talents. Do this for all the bullet points on your resume, including any volunteer work, relevant coursework, or class projects.

3. Based on the talents you have listed next to your bullet points, determine if you are maximizing your Functional Value by leveraging your talents to build skills. Is there collaboration? For example, if your top five influential talents include being *creative* and *curious* like Sam, are those connected to or disconnected from the list of primary talents you just assigned to the bullet points on your resume? Let's say the majority of the bullet points on your resume reflect experiences that would be supported by the talents of being methodical, logical, and detail-oriented, and those talents are *not* on your top five list, then you are quite possibly writing with the "wrong hand" and should consider a recalibration between your talents and skills moving forward. This process can help you identify what you need to change to get on your own right path, a path where you are maximizing your Functional Value. If you find that there is collaboration, then you are likely writing with the "correct hand."

If you don't have a resume, you need to put one together! You will, of course, need it when you apply for the right-fit jobs or internships you identify later in the book, but a resume also provides you with an opportunity to document where you've been professionally and where you are today so you can make any adjustments to fully leverage your talents. There is an unending supply of resume examples online. If your college has a career center, go to its website for good examples and take advantage of a career advisor or counselor's expertise to help you develop a resume that best reflects your Functional Value.

Check In . . .

Recognizing, respecting, and making the most of your talents, nurturing them as Hemingway would have advised Fitzgerald, is what I want you to do. Don't discount what you are innately good at simply because it might be different than what others are good at. At the beginning of this chapter I said *the world is a better place when everyone's individual talents are employed*. You can make it better by using your talents to build skills that will maximize your efforts and abilities throughout your career. Celebrate the unique pattern of dust on your wings—it's part of who you are and who you will become.

4

Defining Your Image Value

"My life is my message."
—Mahatma Gandhi

On March 13, 1924, an article titled "Be Proud of What You Do" appeared in the *Crockery and Glass Journal*, a retail trade periodical published between 1894 and 1953. In the article, Samuel W. Weyburn, the president of Dry Goods Corporation, addressed employees of one of his subsidiary companies, Adoin & Co. He said, "There is not a finer thing in achieving success than to be proud not only of your calling, but of the particular organization engaged in that calling, and of your particular job in it."

I came across this nugget one day while doing research about leadership styles across the centuries; I was amazed to find a photo of the original article. Spoken almost a century ago, this message, sadly, has gotten lost over time as people increasingly ignore the importance of being proud of what they do and where they do it as they chase after success. I think this can be particularly true for new college graduates. Pride in what you do is an important part of finding a right fit. I actually believe it's even more relevant today, because we have access to so much imagery and information through technology that influences gratification.

Consider that the more we can see, online and through social media, the more options we have to factor in to who we want to be in the world. The flip side is that having many options may lead us to be hypercritical of ourselves as we compare our lives to others'. This is a conversation I have had many times with both undergraduate and graduate students, who often compare themselves to their peers. In this case the opportunity to see so much information is both the proverbial blessing and a curse. In the age of information it means we need to be as clear as possible about who we want to be both professionally and personally. It's one reason why I believe this last point has become so important in creating a right fit for new graduates—it actually sets into motion the force necessary to generate the intrinsic motivation that the Working *You* system is built around. Your Image Value matters and should factor into your career decision-making system.

This is why I chose this chapter's opening quote from Gandhi, a man who changed the face of international leadership by heading India's successful campaign for independence from British rule, inspiring movements for freedom and civil rights across the globe. Gandhi was true to who he wanted to be in the world and the image he wanted to represent, and through his commitment to nonviolent resistance he found that authentic connection between his life and his message.

Your Image Value is made up of two attributes:

#1: Your Ego

#2: Your Reputation

Remember that for our purposes, ego is tied to a feeling of accomplishment and pride in what you do and where you do it. In that sense, as we discussed earlier in the book, this first part of your Image Value point is derived from an internal source. Your reputation, on the other hand, is derived from an external source. Your Image Value is about having a job that creates harmony between how you want the world to see you and how it actually sees you in order to authentically experience self-importance, self-worth, self-respect, and self-esteem. *Feeling good about yourself matters.*

By combining these internal and external forces authentically to reflect the image that is uniquely important and valuable to you, you support and facilitate the image of who you want to be in the world in an empowering way. Whenever you can combine these two attributes and connect them to the correlating External Identity of your employer—you galvanize your motivation to do what you do in a formidable way.

The Value of Your Image: #1 Your Ego and #2 Your Reputation

Dr. Wilhelm Hofmann is a professor at the University of Chicago who studies social and personality psychology, including executive functioning. German educated, his work and collaborations span the globe. One of his research findings that I find most fascinating directly relates to the importance of the last You Point we are addressing in this chapter. Dr. Hofmann found that *pride* as a human emotion increased both individual effort and the attainment of success. The experiment he conducted called on subjects to respond throughout the day via text messages to communicate whether or not they had been successful in avoiding any "temptations" they consciously sought to elude, like drinking too much alcohol, eating too much, or even procrastinating. People in the study identified temptations they perceived as negatively impacting their success in achieving their personal goals. What Dr. Hofmann found was that the pride people experienced when they were successful in avoiding their identified temptations not only increased the likelihood that they would continue to avoid these temptations in the future, but it also fostered a sense of diligence and dedication that made them *value* their future more. This is an important concept to consider in finding a job you love after graduation, because believing in the *value* of your own professional future and working with diligence and dedication to live your best life are indispensable ingredients to career success. Why? Because they are also by-products of intrinsic motivation.

Working *You*: Identifying Your Image

What about your job will make you proud to tell people where you work and what you do? How do you want the world to see you and who do you want to become? For your Image Value point, we will address its two parts, ego and reputation, at the same time. As I mentioned earlier, I found that when the *value of our image* in the world of work becomes part of the powerful force between who we are and what we do, it can propel us forward—and upward—at warp speed.

Making a Difference in Columbus

〜〜〜

When I interviewed Jordan Pearson, he was about to graduate from Ohio University with a bachelor's degree in information and telecommunications systems with minors in business and political science. Jordan had also served as a specialist in the Ohio Army National Guard throughout college, having joined as a senior in high school. His mom had been on active duty in the Persian Gulf, and he was inspired by her service and wanted to similarly serve his state and country. He tries to be fiscally responsible, and if you serve in the Ohio Army National Guard while in college, the guard will pay full tuition at Ohio state schools. In addition to being a full-time student and serving in the National Guard, Jordan also worked in the university's career center. That's more than a full plate.

When I asked him about his plans after graduation, Jordan was pleased to report that he had accepted an offer with a midsize technology solutions company in Columbus, Ohio. I was curious about the path he'd taken to get there, because he sounded really excited about his new job. I definitely saw him as one of that small group of happy students graduating with a job he loved. Jordan said, "I had an internship with a huge company that paid really well last summer.

Going into the internship, I thought it was everything I wanted in a full-time job after I graduate—lots of new people, a well-known technology brand, and the money was definitely there. But then I started thinking that having a job at that company in a big city after college, and doing it full-time, wasn't exactly how I wanted to contribute to the world or who I wanted to be."

When I asked him to explain the difference between the fit he experienced at his internship and the fit he believes he will have at the company he's joining after graduation, he was crystal clear. "What makes me really proud about my new job is the chance to make a difference through technology in Columbus. The company I'm going to work for only serves Columbus, and contributing to making things better right here is important to me. I didn't necessarily feel that connection at the large company. This job is contributing to who I want to be right now."

Feeling proud of what you do and where you do it is directly related to how you define success. It's an important concept to consider, because after all, we work to achieve something, and that something is arguably our definition of success. So of course the next question I asked Jordan was, "How do you define success?"

Here is his response: "Success is being able to love what you do and stay motivated. Loving your job in the context of your personal mission statement is important to me. I'm not saying for everybody, but for me. People told me to take the job at the big company because it paid a lot of money. Money is important, but there's more to success for me. Taking pride in my job because of how it connects to my mission statement, who I want to be and what I want to accomplish, is going to help me persevere when things don't go well. There's a deeper meaning that I'm looking for in my career, and it goes beyond money. I want to be proud of the people I work with too. If I'm proud of them, I will be proud of myself."

Jordan gets the importance of his Image Value, and he said it better than I could ever write it.

To get clarity on the image you want to have, first think about who impresses you as a professional and who you aspire to be like. It may be someone you know—for example, a current or past boss or a mentor. It may also be a relative, or even someone you don't know but have heard about. It may be someone famous. Whether they are heading up a Fortune 100 company or making a difference for ten people in a start-up, who impresses you? They don't even have to be in a field that's interesting to you. This point is all about *image*.

1. List a minimum of five people who impress you and you aspire to be like. Think about these people in the context of who they are as working professionals. This is the primary lens I want you to look through as you define both parts of your Image Value, so keep that perspective in full view.

2. Think about *why* they impress you and what the "image qualities" are relative to the personal traits and behaviors they project as professionals. Typically, the traits and behaviors we admire in others often represent traits and behaviors that we would like to be seen as possessing too—even if we don't want to admit this or perhaps consider them too frivolous for ourselves. For this part of your journey, I want you to go there. This question will help you dig deeper to create a

complete picture of who you want to be in the world—personally and professionally—not just today, but also over time. See yourself walking in their shoes; how would it feel if it were you instead of them? My guess is that it would feel good. And it's this exact feeling of "goodness" that ensues when your ego and reputation work together in a right fit.

3. Create a list of descriptors from your five people that collectively sum up the image you want others to use to describe *you*, using them as benchmarks and then going beyond their achievements to describe the image that's important to you (see Cara and Sam's template examples for guidance). Think of how you want people to describe you if they were asked these same questions about you— particularly as a working professional. When you put everything together, this list represents tangible criteria you will use later to make sure the job you take supports the image that's important to you. Remember, this isn't about being a narcissist or a jerk—it's about meeting a human need and being proud of what you do and where you do it. It's simply about being you in a way that matters to *you*. It's about self-esteem and all of the other important "self" words that you deserve to experience.

Image Template: Cara

Who impresses me and who do I aspire to be like?

Misty Copeland

Jessica Alba

Bobby Murphy

Sheri Canfield (my aunt)

Michelle Obama

Why do they impress me, and what are the *image qualities* (personal traits and behaviors) they project that I admire?

Misty Copeland—Because she is the first African American woman to become a principal dancer in the American Ballet Company, considered one of the best ballet companies in the country. Because she overcame all kinds of personal obstacles to reach her dream, and because now she is helping other kids real-ize their dreams. Because she is a beautiful human being who inspires others and works hard. Because she is fierce.

Jessica Alba—Because she is making a difference and taking risks in business. Because she fights for other women. Because she is powerful. Because she stands up to injustice. Because she is a good mother. Because she is maxi-mizing her opportunities in life. Because she is self-made. Because she is super-smart. Because she is super-talented.

Bobby Murphy—Because he is innovative and smart. Because he is the second youngest billionaire of all time because he is innovative and smart. Because he didn't let his first business failure stop him from trying again with Snapchat. Because he wasn't born rich and is self-made. Because he started a founda-tion to help other people get an education and also promotes the value of the arts in the world.

continued

Sheri Canfield—Because she believes in herself and loves her family unconditionally. Because she never gives up. Because she listens. Because she helps other people live their best life. Because she is a teacher.

Michelle Obama—Because she doesn't back down when she believes in something. Because everyone knows how smart she is. Because she is one of the most famous women in the world and she is still real. Because she is both tough and classy. Because she will admit her flaws. Because she wants others to be as successful as she is.

Descriptors that summarize the image I want others to use to describe me:

Powerful and influential. Smart. Classy. Strong and caring. I want to be seen as being involved in the world. I want to be recognized as being self-made and achieving at an A+ level. I want to be seen as someone who isn't afraid to take risks in order to excel and make a difference.

Image Template: Sam

Who impresses me and who do I aspire to be like?

Elon Musk

Serena Williams

Reid Hoffman

James Cross (my brother)

Simon Sinek

Why do they impress me and what are the *image qualities* (personal traits and behaviors) they project that I admire?

Elon Musk—Because he is a visionary and a risk taker. Because some people think he is a mad creative genius. Because he is a change agent. Because he has accomplished goals no one else has accomplished. Because he dances to his own beat.

Serena Williams—Because she knows she is good. Because she isn't afraid to stand up to tennis umpires. Because she is strong-minded. Because she is her own person and sets her own standards. Because she never gives up.

Reid Hoffman—Because he is a pioneer. Because he impacted millions of people with LinkedIn. Because he believes that when you keep learning, you keep growing. Because he isn't afraid to mix up ideas. Because he is an independent thinker.

James Cross—Because he overcame a life-changing illness. Because he is a warrior and a rebel. Because he loves his family. Because I can always count on him to tell me the truth. Because he is ingenious. Because he is my hero.

Simon Sinek—Because he is imaginative. Because he is a world-class explainer. Because he turns on light bulbs for people.

Descriptors that summarize the image I want others to use to describe me:

Bold entrepreneur. Inventor. Leader. Turns dreams into realities. Creative innovator. Ethical rule breaker. World-class success story. Stands up to bullies. Fighter.

Check In . . .

Gandhi said, "My life is my message." *What is your message?* Thinking about who you want to be and how your job can contribute to delivering that message to the world provides you with a luxury most people don't have in their lives. Being proud of both your *calling* and your employer will create a commodity in your life that goes far beyond self-esteem. Again and again, I hear from people who love their job—recent graduates and seasoned professionals alike—that they actually feel like they're where they're supposed to be. The people who have experienced what most would consider to be great accomplishments felt this sense of professional providence throughout their careers. I honestly believe that if you have this last You Point—your Image Value— plugged into the External Identity of your employer, you will be ready to reach the top of Maslow's pyramid where you are living your best life. Don't sacrifice this commodity as you begin looking for a job that's right for you. It's part of being rewarded for the value you bring to the workplace, and it will make it all so sweet.

5

A New Meaning of Work

*"Life is occupied in both perpetuating itself
and in surpassing itself; if all it does is maintain
itself, then living is only not dying."*
—Simone de Beauvoir

Right now, as you are reading this book, there is a transformation taking place in the world of work that is changing how people seek and find meaning through their jobs. This change absolutely impacts your path as you move from defining your own unique value to connecting it with fields, companies, and roles where you are rewarded for that value. Nowhere is this new meaning of work more apparent, at least to me, than among college students, and it undeniably factors into the equation of success. After all, the *sum* of meaning that you take away from your job—in the present and over time—is part of that equation. So let's take a brief but important side trip to get a closer look at how the meaning of work is changing and the catalyst behind its current transformation. This chapter ends with an opportunity for you to define what success means for you—and doing so will help guide you to finding jobs in Step Two that create the most meaningful *meaning*.

While it's true that I think this change in how people seek and find meaning through their jobs is more evident among college students than in other demographics, I also find this type of transformation happening with others. The older you are, the *less evident* the changes, but they are still there and making an impact. My takeaway is that the meaning of work is pretty much changing for everyone, but as college students, you're simply closer to the catalyst behind the change, which I will do my best to deconstruct.

As we have already discovered, setting yourself up in a right fit after college has to be all about *you* in order for the job to be intrinsically motivating. This is a very different approach to career planning, because historically the focus has mostly been on the employer. For example, in the past, job hunting looked like this: *Who does the employer want me to be? Let me find the job first and then I'll think about how I can change my resume and my story to meet their needs.* It was very much a "Pick me, Pick me" mind-set. But the power dynamics in the world of work have changed—connection and transparency have turned old mind-sets and paradigms upside down.

Remember the truism "Information is power"? Think about this enduring truth in terms of the workplace and the role it plays in how we seek and find meaning at work. Consider that, historically, company leaders held all the power. As employees, we were often dependent on our boss to inform us about what was going on in our field, in the marketplace, and within the workplace environment itself. I couldn't navigate to Glassdoor to see if I was being paid fairly. I couldn't network with people through LinkedIn to compare different employers. We had to take the word of the boss about the financial health of the company, whether good or bad, because we had no place to go to fact-check. And we certainly never knew about company leaders personally, because, well, we weren't living in a transparent time.

All that has changed. Today, employees have access to the same "power" of information that was traditionally held almost solely by employers. Today, college students and recent graduates are able to access the same level of information-based power that was once reserved only for employers. In fact, this is a paradigm shift that I encourage you to take advantage of by accessing all of the field- and company-specific information available to you as you fully define each Employer Point for potential right-fit jobs.

But think of this shift from a more macro perspective in terms of your instantaneous access to information about virtually everything that exists in the world beyond the workplace and its relationship to employee empowerment. For example, if I asked you a question about the capital of a minuscule country or the life expectancy of a panda, you could pull out your phone, tablet, or laptop and, thanks to the internet, answer me within seconds. Ask "How are Cheetos made?" and you'll immediately be linked to an article that tells you how to "turn a hunk of cornmeal into a knobby Cheeto." Yes, I tried it, and it works. Having access to incalculable amounts of information is a powerful feeling, no matter how silly the question posed.

In the contemporary world of work, whenever you want and wherever you are, you can be connected to highly specific layers of information about your field, your employer, and even previously hidden layers, such as the personal lives of corporate leaders. And therein lies the catalyst creating the change in how people seek and find meaning through their jobs. Because information is power, empowered employees cannot be coerced into engagement; you have to be *motivated* into engagement, which requires that your job is meaningful in a different and more personal way than it ever was for your parents or grandparents. I believe this fact is one key reason why the Working *You* system has struck a chord for my students. There is perhaps no greater or more sustaining source of professional meaning than intrinsic motivation, which is exactly what the system's right fit produces. As college students and recent graduates, your view of the world has undeniably been "zooming out" since you were born, and as a result, the meaning of work looks very different from this new, *empowered* vantage point. Let's continue our side trip for one more block, because as future leaders yourselves, I think you may find it valuable.

Zooming Out

Long before enhanced connection and the information age began expanding our view of the world, John Glenn, the first American to orbit Earth in 1962, expressed the power of this expanded view when he said, "I don't know what you can say about a day where you have seen four beautiful sunsets." Whether our vehicle to an expanded view is connection and information or a NASA spacecraft, zooming out changes more than just the vantage point from which we view the world. It changes our perceptions, beliefs, and values. The process outlined on the following page is rewiring how people seek and find meaning through work in today's professional landscape.

1. Continuous *connection* allows you to consume mass amounts of information at any time of day about everything related to your job. The result of all this information is targeted knowledge—and it exponentially increases your state of professional awareness and *empowerment* because it spectacularly expands your view of what you do and where you do it.

2. As a result of this increased awareness and empowerment, your *perceptions*—what you think and feel about what you see and do at work—shift and change.

3. When your perceptions begin to shift and change, your beliefs and values get rewired in the process. You then use these beliefs and values to find meaning along an individual career path in pursuit of your own unique definition of success.

While breaking down what is truly an evolutionary push forward in how people find meaning through their work and achieve success, I found it particularly telling that the word *perception* is defined in the dictionary as a "capacity for comprehension" and *belief* as a "conviction of truth." Because after all, without comprehension, there can arguably be no conviction. Thus it makes perfect sense that when you change your metaphorical "seat" and view the world from this extended vantage point, what you think, feel, and ultimately believe and value about work is also going to shift and change.

Here's a sports metaphor I use to explain this new seat: It's like watching a baseball game from the announcer's booth versus behind the dugout. From the announcer's booth, you have a seat that provides additional information about the game because of its vantage point—information that has the power to change both your *comprehension* and *convictions* about how the game is being played. On the other hand, if you were watching the game from the lower elevation of the dugout, from what is literally a ground-level view, the information you take in is significantly reduced due to the limited line of sight. From this ground-level view, there is a dramatic reduction in one's state of awareness and informational "power" about what is going on in the game. Therefore, the meaning you experience through the game changes, depending on where you sit.

Last, consider that *meaning* is defined in the dictionary as an "inner" or "true interpretation" of what you see. This is exactly why changing your seat changes more than just your vantage point. It changes your perceptions, your beliefs, and your values—and, as a result, your path to meaning and the achievement of your success. Today, this process of zooming out and seeing the world of work from an extended vantage point transforms how people find meaning in their professional lives, because connection has given all of us ordinary human beings a ticket to a seat with the power of an aerial view.

Defining Success

In order to achieve success, you must first define what success looks and feels like for *you*. Why is this important? Because if you can't properly define success, it's almost impossible to map out the best route to get there. Think of it this way: When you open a maps app on your phone, it doesn't read your mind and provide you with directions to get where you want to go—at least not yet. *You have to enter the destination.* By defining your destination of success, you gain important insights about your beliefs and values to plug into the Working *You* system as a guide to finding meaningful jobs.

John Wooden, the illustrious UCLA basketball coach who stacked up more than six hundred victories and ten national titles, said, "Success is peace of mind, which is a direct result of self-satisfaction in knowing you did your best to become the best you are capable of being." Maya Angelou, the great poet laureate, said, "Success is liking yourself, liking what you do, and liking how you do it." Richard Branson has said his definition of success is, "The more you're actively and practically engaged, the more successful you will feel." And Arianna Huffington has said that we need a third metric for success beyond money and power that includes "well-being, wisdom, wonder, and giving."

If you define success simply as winning, as being about only money or possessions, or using only quantitative measurements without any qualitative ones, you are actually shortchanging yourself. My best advice is to use both quantitative and qualitative measures as you define your own meaning of success. As I said at the outset of this chapter, for our purposes success is realized through the *sum* of meaning that you take away from your job. It's the ultimate professional bounty, and most people never stop to honestly consider what bounty they're seeking. But you'll be the exception.

The Power of an Aerial View and Getting an MBA

Gaby Omenn took my career class as part of her MBA program. After reading her very candid and honest answers to a midterm about professional meaning and how she measures success, I knew it would be important to include her story here. Gaby brings to life the impact of the new power dynamic that an aerial view of the world of work provides.

She worked as a teacher after receiving her undergraduate degree in religion, then later moved on to a role in human resources with one of the world's largest tech companies—a company that has unquestionably contributed to supplying the seemingly infinite amounts of information-based power I have just been discussing. While working at the tech company, Gaby began to feel less satisfied and to take away less meaning from her work. "My view of success has shifted over time: in my first few years out of college, I was wrestling with the effects of feeling as though I didn't perform as well as I should have in order to achieve success in my career. At that time, I defined success pretty comparatively: I wanted to reach the same level of success as my peers over the next few years, working at organizations that had strong name-brand recognition and getting enough promotions to feel like I could reach financial stability

and establish myself as having *made it*. That didn't happen during my time as a teacher, but it did happen when I left and went to a big name-brand tech giant. At first, I felt valued and well-respected by my peers, and I had achieved the financial freedom to travel and buy nice things. It was a welcome departure from my non-profit days in education! However, I still was left wanting, because the meaning I took away each day wasn't necessarily adding up to the success I was really after. For example, the company I was working for is a *massive* company, and being one employee out of seventy thousand (and counting), my scope felt small. I felt like I wasn't making enough of an impact. But I had a job that wasn't stressful or taxing, working on average thirty-five to forty hours a week and getting paid more than I ever had in my life. At a surface level it was amazing for the personal stage I was in: transitioning to motherhood. However, I wasn't motivated. Despite meeting the milestones I had set for myself, I was watching the clock tick by every day and started to feel like I was losing ground."

After having her first child, she made the decision along with her husband to go back to graduate school and get her MBA—and a new career path that would hopefully provide her with greater meaning. "It was during this time that I realized my success metrics had evolved, because what was meaningful to me had evolved. In fact, I received an internship offer to return to the company I left while pursuing my MBA, and I turned it down for a more obscure company in a different role."

When I asked Gaby if she thought this expanding view of the world of work played a role in her "underwhelming feeling" about her job, she said, "It's funny, because when we talked about this in class a lightbulb went off, and I started thinking about what was different for me now versus when I first left college. I have to say that the more I came to know about my field, the less convinced I became that I was in the right place. Seeing more isn't a formula for being content. It's the opposite. Beyond just seeing more as the spark that can change how you define satisfaction, it seemed to change how I think about the role of work in my life. These aren't the same metrics I used to have, and it isn't all attributable to being a few years older and becoming a parent. It's more than that. But seeing more also creates an opportunity for introspection, because there's a simultaneous realization that I can be more than I am today. If you are driven and goal-oriented, then your benchmarks for what's meaningful get expanded too."

The three main tenets that Gaby now defines as being the fuel for professional and personal meaning are: 1) The work needs to be challenging and core to the business. In prior roles, she felt her job was ancillary, and she wants to be closer to making key strategic decisions for the organization. 2) She wants to feel that when she reaches the upper levels within the company, her potential is realized. On this point, she told me, "When I've looked at the leadership I've had in the past, their suite of responsibilities hasn't inspired me, and I haven't wanted to work toward getting promoted to their positions. I guess it's true, I could see so much about what they do and who they are that it hasn't been enough to keep me really motivated and inspired." And 3) she wants a strong cultural fit while having the flexibility to be present for her family. In deciding to start a family, she made a conscious choice that her life's work would include raising strong, involved citizens of the world, and she needed the space to do that well during the next several years as her children grow up.

Gaby also told me that now and moving forward in her professional life, when assessing current and future career paths she's going to use these three tenets as guides to lead her to a level of meaning that will keep her moving forward toward her own definition of success.

Taking the time to define what success means to you can help guide you as you make career decisions now and in the future, including identifying the fields, companies, and roles that will create the most *meaning* for you.

So how does this play out in real life? Every key professional decision you make will either take you closer to or further away from your definition of success. Every one. Always. Of course, how you define meaning will change over the years as you grow and evolve—as it should. But it's not important what that definition of success will or won't be years into the future. You need a destination that's relevant to you today, and that's where we are going next in the Working *You* system. For example, if you want to be a partner in a global consulting firm, then achieving that goal would be part of how you would define success. If being loved and cared about by family and friends is how you define success, then include this too.

To begin, consider these ten questions:

1. What are you driven to achieve?
2. What do you most often daydream about when thinking about the future?
3. What does your life look like when you are in a job you love after college?
4. Who do you envision yourself becoming in ten years? In twenty years? In thirty years?
5. What have you done in your life that resulted in feeling successful?
6. How do you want to feel about your work when you go to sleep at night?
7. What do you want others to say about you as a colleague? As an employee? As a boss?
8. What type of lifestyle do you want to live?
9. What do you want to see as the impact of your work?
10. What would be the biggest regret in your life in ten years as you see it now?

Working *You*: Defining Success

In your own words, define what success means to you. Your responses to the preceding questions should help you gain clarity about this important theme of success. For example, are you making a positive difference in the lives of others, making a lot of money, respected by your family and colleagues, known as a leader in your field, changing how people live, and so on? Take a look at Cara and Sam's completed templates and follow their lead.

Then write down how you might use this definition of success in assessing current and future career paths. For example, would a professional role where you would be asked to represent the company at meetings and conferences contribute to "feeling like you are a leader in your field"? You will use your answers to this question to kick-start the next section of the book as you build your own map to your destination of success.

Success Template: Cara

1. What does success mean to me?

For me, success is a big mixture of a lot of things that all relate back to what I define as fulfilling my purpose. In this sense, it's more about me than about other people, but other people play a role in how I would define myself as successful. Right now, thinking about what life will be like after college, success will mean that I can take care of myself financially and not be stressed out, but it will also mean that I am making the most of my potential, if not every day, then more days than not. Not being successful would feel like I'm wasting my time and sort of swimming in place, treading water. Success to me is about moving forward and continuing to discover what I'm capable of doing and how I can make an impact. Success also means that I am taking

continued

other people with me to maximize their potential too. I see success as being recognized for my contributions. Definitely through promotions and raises, but I also want public recognition for being a leader and changing what I want to change in a positive way. Being recognized by others for improving the world in whatever way I have the opportunity and power to do will definitely make me feel successful when I go to bed at night. Success is also about growth, and seeing my bank account grow at the same time my impact on others grows will mean something to me. It's also about working in an environment that's aesthetically appealing and feeling good about myself because of my surroundings when I walk through the doors in the morning.

In ten years, I want to definitely be able to look back and see a lot of positive changes in my wake, where I have changed the world because of the path I traveled. Being able to travel and live a comfortable life is also a sign of success for me, and being able to live that life with my friends and family is going to be fundamentally important. Success and freedom go hand in hand for me. The biggest regret that I would see for myself in the future would be not believing in myself enough to take chances that could make the difference between being triumphant and feeling cheated.

2. How can I use my definition of success to assess current and future career paths?

I feel like my definition of success can be a positive thing to keep in mind because it can help me determine whether I'm staying true to myself or taking a job—or not taking a job—because it's the easy way out. A job that is going to give me some autonomy to make decisions, pay me what I feel I'm worth, and make me feel like I'm contributing to others in a way that will resonate with me is what I now see as something I deserve. I also see that I need to work with people who have high standards and share my philosophy of not wanting to feel cheated in any way in life. I'm definitely going to be using all of this as a litmus test for whatever company I think about working for, because to make my definition of success a reality, I know I will need to be on a team with other people like me.

Success Template: Sam

1. What does success mean to me?

I define success based on three considerations.

Having unlimited potential: This is about living a life that doesn't keep my capacity muffled or muted because someone else is calling the shots. Success for me can't be based on another person's fears or insecurities or lack of vision. Whether my vision makes a ton of money or even becomes a reality, not being able to pursue it would be failing. I want to have control over how far I go based on my own creativity and hard work. Creating a career and a life where I can go as far or as far afield as I need to go is, in my mind, being a success. I don't want to be limited to pay grades based on how long I work somewhere or how old I am. I want it to be based on my contribution to the company and maximizing my own capability.

Being known as a nonconformist change agent: Being ordinary is another way I would define being a failure. I don't want to be boxed in by labels. Success for me is about doing things better than they're being done today and connecting dots in ways that other people haven't done or can't do. I get satisfaction for being seen as a leader because I bring ideas and strategies to the table no one else has brought before. I think this goes back to being motivated by nonjudgmental environments and people. I like risks because I think that's really the only way big changes in the world happen, and I'm not afraid of the downside of risk. Not having things always turn out the way you wanted is just life. But that's also part of being known as a change agent. There were a lot of disappointments before the first moon landing, and there will be a lot of disappointments before people walk on Mars.

My definition of success also pulls into play the effects that being a change agent have on the world. I would feel successful at the end of my life if people I never met are living their lives differently, and by differently I mean different in a positive way, because of my work. I feel like everybody cares about making a difference for people they know, and that's definitely important. But I want to make a difference for people I don't know, because to me, that would mean that I've been a real change agent.

continued

Achieving things in the future I haven't even dreamed of in the present: This one is key for me because it means I'm not stagnating, which I think would be the worst thing that could happen in my career and in my life. Thinking about this concept of success means not tying myself too much to benchmarks, because I want to be open to where my brain and others' brains can take me. Who knows what things might be possible twenty years from now, and I want to always be open to the next adventure and the next possibility. Being able to go in new directions in my career and in my life because of changes that will happen in the world would definitely mean I'm a success, because it would mean I'm not stagnating and am seeing potential in new places.

2. How can I use my definition of success to assess current and future career paths?

If I keep these three definitions of success in mind as I start my career after school and then moving forward, I believe I will make decisions and go in directions where each of these can be part of my career trajectory. If I don't feel like these three are going to be part of the makeup of that job, then I don't want to go there, because it will be the wrong direction. I know I need to keep moving, because that's who I am. I see these three definitions of success helping me to keep moving as long as I don't let them go. I never really thought about defining success in this way before, and I think it will help me make better decisions in my life at work and also in my personal life. It's about who I am and the freedom to be whoever I want to be in all areas of my life, and that reaches across both work and home.

Check In . . .

In the opening quote for this chapter, acclaimed French writer, academic, phi-
losopher, and feminist Simone de Beauvoir references the path to success when
she says, "Life is occupied in both perpetuating itself and in surpassing itself:
if all it does is maintain itself, then living is only not dying." Think about your
life and career path as transformative; each decision you make about where
you work takes you closer to or further from your definition of success. As
the meaning of work evolves and changes, leverage these changes to grow
and "surpass" who you were yesterday. Recognizing what generates meaning
in your life is key to this equation. As I said earlier in the book, we are all working to achieve something and success is arguably that something. Now that
you have thought about what *your* definition of success looks and feels like,
you will hopefully have a greater stake in the next step we are about to take
together, which is to identify the fields, companies, and roles that will facilitate
your success. Onward!

STEP TWO

Finding Your Own Right Fit

"We need to do better at putting ourselves first on our own 'to do' list."
—Michelle Obama

I often find that students hit a barrier, right at the point when they need to start exploring potential career paths, because of three primary roadblocks:

- They have no idea which direction to look because they don't recognize that the most important sounds to follow are the sounds originating from their own unique value.
- They are overwhelmed by all that exists in the world of work and don't know how to begin filtering through what feels like an abyss of fields, companies, and roles.
- They let online job sites, family, friends, and fear dictate their path.

We can scratch the first roadblock off the list because you should now have your head (and arms) firmly wrapped around the primary navigational device that will lead you to a right fit: the unique value you've just defined in step one through your three You Points. Think of this value as your bellwether. If you listen to these sounds, they will keep you on the right path.

So let's address the second roadblock. Filtering through the abyss of possible fields, companies, and roles can truly feel like an obstacle course. I've seen it overwhelm a lot of my students. To avoid this particular roadblock, I'll introduce you to a simple and easy-to-use job-search method that's also highly targeted and personal. I call this method 5-5-1 because it encompasses 5 fields, 5 companies in each field, and 1 role associated with each company, ultimately providing you with 25 potential right-fit jobs to explore. The goal of this approach is to take you safely through the obstacle course of jobs so you emerge with your very own tailor-made job bank that represents the most meaningful connections between who you are and what you do. It's an approach designed to mimic a sieve—for any of you who are cooks. It separates out the jobs that probably won't generate a positive force, while saving only the best fits for further exploration. All the rest get washed away. It's ultimately about putting yourself first in your job search in order to find work you love.

That leaves the third roadblock, which is ultimately about staying in charge of your future and not getting pushed down a path that isn't authentically yours. For years I've seen students make wrong decisions because they were listening to the sounds of other people rather than the directional guidance coming from their own value. Think about what Thomas Tran said in chapter 1. He went to law school because his family thought film school wasn't practical. It's why he felt like another species when he first arrived at law school.

Your Personalized Job Bank

If you are in your final year of college or have already graduated (as an under-graduate or graduate student), you will use your job bank to turn your right fits into offers now. If you're currently a freshman, sophomore, or junior, or a graduate student just beginning your studies, your job bank will serve you in two ways. First, as a guide for pursuing internships that can then be turned into full-time work at graduation. And second, as a guide for developing relevant skills through elective classes, volunteer activities, or perhaps even student leadership roles. I'll discuss all of these implementation scenarios based on your own individual timeline in Step Three, starting on page 169.

He had wandered off the path where his creative talent was a sound leading him in the right direction.

I've talked to thousands of college graduates, both on the record and off, including far too many who didn't listen to their own bellwether. When I look at why they didn't listen to who they are, one of the most common causes I see at play is fear. It comes in many forms, and includes being afraid to stand up for your-self and afraid to go against the wishes of those you love for fear they won't love you quite as much—or perhaps at all—if you don't follow *their* sounds instead of your own. It really is about putting yourself first on your to-do list, as suggested by Michelle Obama in this step's opening quote. When it comes to your career and finding a right fit, putting others in the driver's seat of your professional life doesn't make your path *your path*. If you make it their path instead of your own, it can lead to frustrating detours and potholes you don't want to fall into.

I recently made the topic of fear dictating one's career path a classroom discussion for graduate students, but it's just as relevant for undergraduates. Many graduate students have had substantial careers that weren't a right fit and have come back to school to further their education and get on a new path. I ask them to write down their career fears anonymously, and then I select several to discuss in an open forum. We address these fears head-on in our discussion. This practice has become some of the most important time spent in class, because it starts a dialog in which everyone shares their thoughts and experiences to overcome these fears. Since these were all written anonymously, I can share some with you. Hopefully, this might help you realize that you're not alone. Everyone has their own career fears, and they will only have power over you if you don't talk about them.

- Getting an amazing job that I love and not being able to live up to it and then ruining my future in that industry and disappointing people I love.
- I'm afraid that I will be forced into ignoring my talents and have to start writing with the wrong hand for the rest of my career—that I won't be strong enough to stand up for myself.
- Not being able to successfully manage my professional life with my personal life.
- Not following through on next steps that I know are right because I fear success—self-sabotage and feeling like I don't deserve to be successful.
- My biggest career fear is getting stuck because I get lazy and complacent.
- I fear not believing in myself and settling for a job that keeps me from living my best life.
- I'm afraid of being mediocre.
- I fear being disappointed with myself.
- I'm afraid of feeling trapped in a job that's no longer the right job.
- My greatest fear is waking up in an office in thirty years and realizing I didn't make an impact in the world because I took the safe road and settled.

In her book *Do It Scared*, new-media entrepreneur and *New York Times* bestselling author Ruth Soukup asserts that action is the antidote to fear. Soukup talks about how true courage isn't about "not being afraid," but rather about taking action. For our purposes, it's about taking that first step on your career path and putting yourself first even if you're afraid. In her work on this important topic, she discusses how for some people, the fear of not being "good enough" or even "smart" or "talented" enough can prevent them from pursuing their potential. I couldn't agree more.

In addition to being a bestselling author, Soukup also has a top-rated podcast called *Do It Scared* and more than a million subscribers to her weekly newsletter. She shares with her readers and listeners the fears that held her back and impacted the decisions she made in her life. She describes how fear kept her inside a box rather than following her own path in pursuit of her dreams and goals. Her depiction of how fear can prevent us from creating the life we want represents what I've often recognized as a primary reason this third roadblock exists in the first place. The message here, obviously, is don't let fear dictate your career path.

I want you to feel powerful enough—based on all the collective value you bring to the job market—to create the life you want to live, without running into any roadblocks or falling into potholes. In fact, you've already taken action simply by reading this book. Life is short; the goal should be to construct a career that's about you and not about someone else. You deserve it.

The Making of Ourselves

Work, and the meaning we assign to it, plays an important role in what I like to call the making of ourselves. Because work represents such a sizable percentage of the time most adults spend on earth, it should never play a secondary role. Lives supported by jobs that let us be truly valued and rewarded for who we are not only motivate us to work in a way that promotes positive career outcomes, it also brings benefits for employers and for everyone around us. It's a win-win dynamic that I want you to remember when you start hiring your own employees, which will happen a lot sooner than you think when you're in a right fit.

For Employees

There's ample evidence to support the notion that positive validation of an employee's authenticity or truth is connected to a variety of favorable personal and professional outcomes. Some of these include an enhanced capacity to deal with stress and workplace adversity, a greater sense of creativity and superior work processes, the ability to adapt to new work settings, and more effective communication as people relate to each other in positive and productive ways. Research also indicates that authentic identities at work are created in part through our relationships with others, and that work-related

Live Your Legend

~~~

Scott Dinsmore started a movement. In his inspiring TEDx Talk with more than six million views, he encourages people to find a job you "can't not do." After leaving his post at a Fortune 500 company because he wasn't headed in his own right direction, Dinsmore founded Live Your Legend, an online community that, in addition to giving people practical career tools, connects people all around the world to provide encouragement and support for each other's dreams. Live Your Legend became a movement that was indeed driven by a community of people helping each other follow their own path.

In his TEDx Talk, Dinsmore discusses how he came to the realization that many people are climbing a ladder that someone else has told them to climb, and that this ladder is leaned up against the wrong wall or even no wall at all. At the time of his talk, Dinsmore said, 80 percent of people in the world of work don't really like what they do.

Perhaps what makes this message most impactful is what happened a little more than a year after the date of Dinsmore's motivating talk. He tragically died in an accident while climbing Mount Kilimanjaro with his wife. When I play his talk in class, the first thing students comment on is how inspiring Dinsmore's message is and the importance of finding what you "can't not do," based on your own truth. When they learn about his accidental death, the staggering realization that life is indeed short—too short not to travel your own path—almost takes the air out of the room.

We spend way too much time at work—some estimates put that time at around 92,000 hours throughout our lifetime—not to have a career that's based on our own *truth*. It's a message that resonates because the realization that life can change in the blink of an eye is all too real. Creating a life that you love, including a job that you care about and a job that cares about you, isn't something you should even think about as an option—it should be mandatory. I've heard people say that courage is the opposite of fear, while others say faith is the opposite of fear. What I say to you is, *Have the courage to have faith in yourself*. If you have faith that you have what it takes, then you will find the courage to overcome any career fear you may face.

friendships along with daily interaction play a significant role in our own self-construct. It's a point I want you to think about in chapters 7, 8, and 9 as we identify fields, companies, and roles to make sure the meaning you get from work is making you who you want to be.

For Employers

A study by Deloitte LLP shows that employers are "eight times more likely to achieve better business outcomes, six times more likely to be innovative and agile, and two times more likely to meet or exceed financial targets" when employees are essentially Working *You*. Furthermore, young professionals appear to be more attracted to employers who provide workplace environments that positively affirm the personal identities of their employees. This point is made even more significant because by 2025, younger professionals will make up 75 percent of the workforce. It's exactly why creating workplaces in which employees are valued for who they are will not only prove to be good for business but also become a business requirement. Employers who are not *motivating* employees into engagement based on the collective value each employee brings to the workplace will likely risk going out of business. New and ongoing studies continue to back up this line of thinking, suggesting that employers who value both the similarities and differences of individual employees as a vehicle to engage the full potential of their workforce will thrive in this emerging new world of work. LinkedIn's Global Recruiting Trends report, which surveys corporate leaders all around the world, found that the majority of company leaders who took part in the survey are now beginning to recognize that tapping into the authenticity of their employees is indeed good for business. Why? Because the Employer Points represented in the second circle of the Working *You* system will affirm the importance of each employee's unique collective value and drive commitment, innovation, productivity, and loyalty. Win-win begins and ends with right fits for both employees and employers, which is exactly where we are headed to separate out the good fits from the bad fits—for y*ou*.

6

Employer Points and Separating Good Fits from Bad Fits

"Everyone shines, given the right lighting."
—Susan Cain

As Susan Cain observes in the opening quote of this chapter, finding a job that provides you with the right light to shine is what the Employer Points represent in the Working *You* system. Earlier in the book, when we were talking about the value of your personality, I referenced Susan Cain's inspiring and record-breaking Ted Talk about the power of introverts on page 41. In her work, Cain presents an important concept that I waited until now to share about the *entitlement to be yourself*, and the life-transforming effects of having this mind-set. She was of course talking about entitlement as it relates to introverts recognizing that being who they are is powerful. Now, as you start to identify fields, companies, and roles that will provide your own "right light," I want to reinforce how this concept about the "entitlement to be yourself" is at the core of a right fit. It is transformational because when you recognize how powerful you are because of the value you bring to the job market, you will refuse to settle for a bad or even a mediocre fit. Once again, *finding work you love* begins and ends with you. Let's take a deeper dive into what the Employer Points fully represent and how they can make you *shine*. I want you to feel entitled to shine.

Company Character

This first Employer Point correlates with your Human Value point and reflects the degree to which the employer's environment welcomes and respects someone like you, someone with your demographics, personality, and motivational work triggers.

The Company Character of the employer is about the emotional, ethical, and personal qualities that come together to create not only the personality of the company but also the temperament and moral attributes that drive organizational behavior. This means things like hiring practices, evaluation and feedback processes, what type of philanthropy the company may be involved in (if appropriate to the size of the company), and even the honesty, accountability, and courage of company leaders. Company Character is about the humanity of the company across all of these facets. By defining the Company Character of a potential employer, you can determine whether you will likely be welcomed, respected, and *rewarded* for your correlating Human Value.

Success Factors

The second Employer Point correlates with your Functional Value and reflects the degree to which your talents and skills support a successful job performance. In order to determine the Success Factors of a job, you first have to identify a specific role, which we will address in chapter 9. Once you identify a role, you can then categorize the talents and skills needed to be functionally successful, including networking with people who have been successful in the same or a similar role. Adding this layer of on-the-ground intel allows you to determine if you bring the right talents and skills to be rewarded for your Functional Value.

This particular Employer Point isn't called Mediocrity Factors for a reason. Setting yourself up for success requires you to recognize the strengths you functionally bring to the job market to make sure you can meet and go beyond the job's basic requirements. Learning what abilities an employer perceives as responsible for a successful performance in a specific role, such as critical thinking or communication abilities, being a perfectionist or being creative, will allow you to determine if this fit will likely create that necessary positive force.

External Identity

The third Employer Point correlates to your Image Value and reflects the degree to which your ego and reputation needs are met and supported by how the field, company, and role are viewed by others as well as yourself.

The External Identity of the job is based on what its popular impression is in the external world (you can substitute the word *media* if you like, in all of its forms). It's about the mental picture the job creates in the minds of others when you tell them what you do and where you do it. What you're ideally looking for is a match between the symbolism of the field, company, and role that others see when you tell them about it, and who you want to be in the world today and into the future.

One day I was working with an engineering student on this very point about image. She was having a hard time defining what others thought about the job she was thinking about pursuing. We started entering search phrases into Google, like *What do people think of engineers? What do people think of Boeing? What do people think of IBM?* We also entered "image of engineers" and pulled up endless visual images of engineers doing their job across all types of companies. We just sat there for a minute and looked at them. I asked her, "Does this resonate with you? Does this look like who you want to be?" Her answer was a resounding "Yes" as she smiled at the images of professionals representing different genders, ethnicities, and ages. When I asked her why

Superpower

~~~~~~

Garland Fuller is a diversity and inclusion executive for a Fortune 500 company. We met at a conference for real estate leaders in Santa Barbara, where we had both been asked to speak on a panel about the future of the workforce. Sitting next to her on the panel stage, I found myself nodding in agreement with all of her comments. Of course, I asked her if she would share some advice about the importance of recognizing your own value when it comes to setting yourself up for success in a right-fit job, and I was happy that she agreed.

"It's very important for you to be valued for your whole self, especially your demographic identifiers. Your gender, race, ethnicity, age, and sexual orientation are all about how you perceive and respond to the world around you. How you view a situation comes down to experiences that you've had in your life. It's critical that you are not only in a role, but also in an organization whose culture supports and celebrates your individual expression."

"As a cisgendered black woman who identifies as Afro-Latinx, who I am and how I show up in the world needs to be valued by my employer and for me personally; it's actually critical to the job I have in diversity recruiting. It's not only about not succeeding to the level that you deserve as much as it is about the effort you exert to get there.

When you aren't being valued for who you are and able to show up as your whole self at work, so much of your mental and emotional energy is spent working on fitting in. That leaves very little space to take risks for fear of rejection, ridicule, or failure. When you're not contributing as your whole self, you may begin to disengage or potentially withdraw. As a result, the perception is that you are not a leader or a contributing team member, and thus, you aren't considered for promotions or leadership opportunities. It becomes a self-fulfilling prophecy that you aren't succeeding in your role because you're not being yourself. Then you begin to question whether you belong, and oftentimes impostor syndrome sets in."

I asked Garland to offer advice for anyone who may feel they have to work twice as hard as others because of who they are. It's a conversation I've had with many students over the years. At the core of this dynamic is how standing out because of who you are can provide you with a level playing field when you're in a right fit.

Garland said, "As a person of color and a woman, it's an experienced truth that working twice as hard in order to be considered competent and proficient is a reality. Once you've accepted that reality, it's critical to know that your difference is your superpower. Your difference is the lens that allows you to see and experience the world differently. The sooner I learned to embrace my difference and leverage it to my advantage, the more opportunities opened up. It is critical that organizations foster a culture of inclusion, so that all individual differences are not experienced as a threat but as an advantage. It's critical that psychological trust and safety be a given in work environments that value inclusion. Without that trust and safety, diverse employees don't engage, innovate, or openly contribute to their team or organizations at large.

"I'd say you find the right environment by looking at the organization's culture, and whether the values are lived among team members. As far as making a difference for others, it really is taking a genuine interest in your colleagues and getting to know them outside of just their job title. As a manager or director, it's learning how to manage diverse teams and being an inclusive leader. It's leading with compassion and not just focusing on results. If you're a team member, it's realizing that you may want to work on your emotional intelligence to read a room and determine when to speak up and when to listen."

As you move on to explore the other two Employer Points in more detail, hold close the words you just read. Being rewarded for the value of who you are in this first fit point has everything to do with finding an employer with the right Company Character—it's foundational to making the system work for you. Yes, who you are is your "superpower."

she was smiling, she said she thought they all looked "very smart, focused, and full of purpose." These were all descriptions that she wanted to project to the world and be recognized for by others. She agreed that being described as very smart, for example, generated a lot of self-esteem. We also looked at specific company websites to learn what these companies say about themselves in order to determine whether or not they supported who she wanted to be and how she wanted others to view her. It's all about creating that positive force between you and the job, and the force created between your Image Value and the External Identity of the field, company, and role is powerful. Locking in this last connection point between who you are and what you do will create the core of your Working You system, where intrinsic motivation begins to drive your career.

Hiring the Right Talents and Skills

David Ajemian loves his job. As a managing director of Citi Private Bank in Beverly Hills, he is responsible for heading the private bank team in addition to leading the bank's recruiting efforts at USC. If you aren't familiar with the term *private banking*, it represents banking, investments, and other financial services provided to ultra high-net-worth individuals and families (wealth management is actually a subset of private banking). David is a great friend to the cause of helping students find the right job after college and recognizes the importance of hiring people with the right talents and skills. When I asked him about this particular part of a right fit—connecting talents and skills to the Success Factors of the job—he said that he looks for candidates "who have a global citizen mind-set and an abundance of never-ending curiosity and willingness to learn."

One of the college students he recognized as a right fit was Annie Tung. Annie met David when he spoke to my class about the field of private banking and why he loves his job. His message and information resonated with Annie, and she followed up with David for an informational interview. She then applied to and was hired for an internship, which led her to a full-time job offer after graduation. Like David, Annie loves her job, and cites "positivity and being intellectually curious" as talents she has drawn on to be successful in her role. "In my two years at Citi, not only have I had the opportunity to learn from three different teams (banking, investments, and lending), but I've also had the opportunity to work closely with colleagues from different functions and with diverse backgrounds and experiences. This job has given me hands-on experience and exposure to clients, as well as opportunities to develop skills that take advantage of who I am as an individual."

When it comes to hiring people, David feels the following traits separate the right-fit candidates (you might recognize some of these words from the talent word cloud in chapter 3): "a high emotional quotient, Presence (with a capital P), patience, persistence, perseverance, adaptability, curiosity, and a willingness to never stop learning, evolving, and developing."

Assessing how your own talents and skills will support and facilitate a successful job performance in a specific role is key to being rewarded for your Functional Value. It's a necessary part of creating the "right light" in order to shine.

5-5-1: Finding Right Fits and Weeding Out Bad Fits

I designed the 5-5-1 method to make it easy to identify the best right-fit jobs in an individualized way. It's an approach that further serves to personalize your job search, reflecting the importance of who you are in the job market along with your own definition of success. I referred to this method in the previous chapter as a professional sieve. By design it will separate out the good fits from the bad fits, leaving you with only those jobs most likely to create the positive force between your You Points and their correlating Employer Points that generates the game-changing commodity of intrinsic motivation. It's based on a targeted approach revolving around a central theme: *What's interesting to you?* It's a question you will see asked and answered differently at the field, company, and role levels, which, when you put them all together, represent the full picture of what a job is all about.

In the next chapters, we'll start populating your tailor-made job bank by discovering and identifying five fields and five companies in each of those fields that are uniquely interesting to you. Based on how you answer the *What's interesting?* question, you will automatically be weeding out fields and companies that are unlikely to be a right fit. At the end of the process, you will then find twenty-five potential right-fit employers in your job bank and be ready to explore right-fit roles. As you may have guessed, it's your answers to the *What's interesting?* question that will personalize the job bank *for you*.

Check In . . .

Everyone reading this book will have different answers to the question *What's interesting?* Therefore, what you find left in your metaphorical job sieve after you've strained out all the bad fits are the jobs that provide the strongest connection between who you are and what you do. If a job isn't among the jobs left inside the sieve, it isn't interesting enough to pursue, because your Human Value, Functional Value, and Image Value points aren't reflected to the degree they need to be to qualify for further exploration. *It's about finding that right light.* Now, let's dive deeper into the meaning of "interesting" and start populating a job bank in which your "superpower" can work for you. You're worth the work, and I'll be right there in the trenches with you. Let's find the work you love!

7

Finding a Right Field

"Pleasure in the job puts perfection in the work."
—Aristotle

Identifying fields of interest begins with giving yourself permission to consider any field that grabs your attention and that you can categorize as appealing, fascinating, exciting, or stimulating. Think about areas that motivate and engage you, and make your list of fields as long as you want. Where do you go, either mentally or physically, when you have free time and can pursue and experience activities of your choice? Do you love playing or watching sports? Then for our purposes, the *field* of sports would qualify as interesting to you. Do you love technology? Cars? Fashion? Finance? Food? Money? Movies? Music? Real estate? Politics? Science? The stock market? Travel? Video games?

The field level is where you'll begin to weed out jobs that don't have a genuine connection to who you are and find jobs that are much more likely to create a real sense of engagement and motivation because they're already interesting. *You can't have sustained intrinsic motivation without authentic engagement.* A recent survey from Gallup, which surveyed millions of people in more than two hundred countries around the world, found that only 15 percent of respondents report being engaged by their job. *Forbes* found similar results, defining *engaged* as having a "deep connection" to your work. That deep connection starts with a field that is interesting—*to you.*

What's Your Thing?

Giorgio Armani is a billionaire many times over. His clothing brand is known all over the world, and his designs are regularly worn by celebrities from Beyoncé to Lady Gaga to George Clooney. Even Anna Wintour, editor in chief of *Vogue* and widely revered as fashion's ultimate voice, has worn Armani.

Living in a small town outside of Milan, Armani's family endured the harsh challenges of World War II. In an interview with *Harper's Bazaar*, Armani said, "We were poor and life was tough." He added, "The cinema in Milan was a refuge—a palace of dreams—and the movie stars seemed so glamorous." This is where, he said, he "fell in love with the idealized beauty of Hollywood stars." In another interview, Armani talked about how, as a child, he made dolls out of mud. Along with his brother, he put on shows for the family with puppets made of wood and clothing he made from scraps of material found on the street.

After fulfilling his military commitment, he took a temporary job at a high-end department store, designing window displays with the latest fashions. Here, he connected to a field that was his thing—the field of fashion design. He described how, in addition to designing windows, he soon started assisting photographers during fashion shoots. It wasn't long before he was on the sales floor, selling men's clothing, before moving up to buyer. The next step beyond buyer was designer, so he left the store to design for various fashion houses, including a famous men's line of the day named for its stylist, Nino Cerruti. From there, he went out on his own with his own brand, and the rest is history.

Here's why choosing a field based on how you answer the question "What's interesting?" is so important. Do you think Armani would have had this same level of success in another field? Of course, it's impossible to know because it didn't happen, but think about the ultimate outcome in this example. Over the years, Giorgio Armani has designed clothes for more than one hundred films. By the year 2000, the Armani brand was considered the top Italian design house, and in 2019, his personal fortune was estimated at nearly $10 billion. The takeaway? Pay attention to *your thing*—what grabs your attention. Finding a right field is about connecting who you are with what you do in the most

A Field of Fascination

Stephen Anderson studied architecture and real estate as an undergraduate at the University of Southern California, because understanding how cities are built and how people come together to form communities through infrastructure and buildings was *interesting* to him. I first met Stephen as an undergraduate student and have followed his career over the years as he detoured away from what gets his attention, and then came back to it in a powerful way. As a little boy, Stephen had a fascination with maps, globes, and snow globes. He would also build entire cities out of Legos. Interestingly, he never followed the directions that came with the Legos; he made up and built his own fantasy cities, representing what he imagined as perfect places to live.

Growing up in suburban Colorado, Stephen and his sister were competitive skiers. When his parents drove them to events all around the state, what interested him most about these experiences wasn't the competition, but rather "walking the streets of these different urban ski villages and feeling the energy. As a kid, I didn't know why I liked it, I just knew I liked it. Some of my earliest memories are about knowing I wanted to live in a city with that street-level energy."

After receiving his undergraduate degree, Stephen switched jobs a few times, finally settling in Los Angeles. There he worked for a large shopping center developer, but the company wasn't a place where he could really be himself and it impacted his work. "I didn't fully appreciate how important it is to have a job where being gay could be viewed as a strength because it's a valuable part of who you are. At the time, there wasn't what I would call a lot of gay-friendly employers in real estate development and I certainly wasn't working for one. What that meant was that I could never talk about my weekends or vacations in an honest way, and it took a toll. I was always dancing around my personal life, because being gay wasn't okay in that environment."

Deciding that he no longer wanted to be in the closet at work, Stephen networked himself into a government-based management role working in urban redevelopment. "In my job with the City of Los Angeles, for the first time in my career I was welcomed for who I am authentically. My self-confidence skyrocketed. I'd never really worked in an inclusive environment, and it felt great." But when budget cuts came along, Stephen found out that his job was going away. This is where things went off track.

continued

He went to work on the redevelopment of the international terminal at the Los Angeles airport, with responsibility for bringing in retail businesses and negotiating leases. "Sure, I was in real estate in a way, and I could definitely do the job, but I wasn't inspired. It wasn't my thing. And it was only funded for a year, so I knew I had to figure something else out fast. By that time, I had veered pretty far away from what was most motivating to me, building buildings and creating cities. I was becoming more and more unhappy and disconnected, not just with my job, but also with myself. I felt like my career had gone into a cul de sac."

Stephen knew he had to get back on track and decided that graduate school was his best option—but only if it focused exclusively on the field of real estate development in a way that mattered and was interesting *to him*. He was accepted into a one-year master's program in real estate development, then pivoted into a purely development role that allowed him to build projects that impacted how people live in big cities. He shared, "It was night and day, going from being totally uninspired and unhappy to actually looking forward to getting up and going to work every day because I loved what I was doing. I could also be out, be myself, and do what I do best, and for the first time, I started to click with my job in a complete way."

Just a few short years later, Stephen is thriving in his chosen field. "I think a lot of people lose sight of who they really are, because the world has a way of shoving you onto a conveyor belt. The purpose that initially might drive you toward one field or another can get blurred pretty quickly if you don't stay focused on who you are and your own interests and what motivates you. Take the time to discover what that means and do your best to stay true to it. Otherwise you get off course. I'm lucky to have found my way back to work that continues to fascinate me."

powerful way possible. Intrinsic motivation is actually *conceived* at the field level, and that's exactly why we are starting your job bank with fields before companies and roles.

Distinguishing Fields from Roles

So, if you love movies and constantly find yourself linking to websites about the latest indie releases, challenge yourself to explore the field of movies. "Movies?" you might ask. "But I think I want to be an accountant." Let's say you have talents that include being detail-oriented and meticulous, and numbers engage you. It's important to recognize that being an accountant at a film company is a completely different experience than being an accountant at an accounting firm, which may or may not be an employer that represents a right fit. It's quite possible that your Human Value and Image Value points would be rewarded to a much greater degree by the Company Character and External Identity Employer Points at a film company than at an accounting firm. Going in the direction of fields that get your attention pulls into play the key ingredients of your first and third You Points.

In this example, while accounting can definitely be considered as a field, I don't want you to begin the 5-5-1 method by boxing yourself in too much with a role—we'll get there. I want you to think of fields as more experience based than function based, because when we do get to roles, you will specifically address job functions via roles (job titles) like "accountant" or "consultant." That said, if you love accounting and articles about accounting always get your attention, there's nothing wrong with listing it as a field.

Here's another example to bring this distinction to life. A few years ago, I had a student who loved fashion. She devoured the latest fashion magazines the minute they came out online or in print. She knew all the notable designers, emerging and celebrated, past and present—*it was just her thing.* As she approached graduation, she had two job offers in marketing roles, and both companies were about as far away from fashion as you could get. She came into my office very troubled because one of these employers had upped its offer to get her to sign—a move that would make most students downright giddy.

She told me she felt trapped just by thinking about going to work in either of these companies. Why? Because she didn't care about the products the companies produced. While both companies were listed on the Fortune 100, they did not produce glamorous products—and again, fashion and glamour were her thing. I thought again about that group of happy new graduates who love their jobs and remembered that each of them is personally connected to the product or service their employers produce. This is what makes a field *interesting* for our purposes in finding right fits and weeding out bad fits. *So what's interesting to you?*

Working *You*: Identifying Right Fields

It's time to make your own list of interesting fields. Remember, make the list as long as you want. List any field that grabs your attention and is appealing, fascinating, exciting, or stimulating. In other words, *what's your thing?*

Try not to filter your answers through the lens of an actual company or role, even if you already have one in mind. You'll get there in the next two levels. The 5-5-1 method works best if you go from the macro *field* level to the micro *role* level, step by step. With that in mind, free yourself up from what many would describe as a traditional career-planning state of mind and write down every field that qualifies as your thing, even if it feels far-fetched as a job.

Then, note *why* each field is interesting. These added details will give you more clarity once you start to rank the fields on your list.

Finally, score your fields on a scale of 1 to 5, with 5 representing *very interested*. To do this, assign three separate numbers to each field based on how you answer the following three questions:

Q1. How interested am I in watching a TV show, reading an article, exploring a website, or engaging in a conversation about this field?

Q2. If I had an hour of free time to devote to experiences that revolve around the product, services, or ideas related to this field, how interested am I in giving up other activities I enjoy to engage with a product or service related to this field? (For example, if golf is an identified field because it's simply your thing, how interested are you in giving up time reading, going to the gym, playing the piano, hiking, and so on to play a round of golf?)

Q3. If I could shadow the CEO of a leading company in this field, how interested am I in giving up time with my best friends to do this? (For example, if technology always gets your attention and is a field on your list, how interested are you in learning more about the CEO who created your favorite app?)

Once you're finished assigning a score to each of these three questions, total up your answers to get one score for each field, and then rank them from highest to lowest. In Cara and Sam's template examples to follow, you can see how this plays out.

Your goal is to identify your top five most interesting fields. If there's a tie for fifth place, use your gut instinct to decide which field is *more your thing.* There won't be a bad answer.

Once you have ranked your top five most interesting fields, move ahead to the next chapter, where you'll identify companies in each of these fields that are personally *interesting* to you. Any fields that didn't make it into your top five, particularly those that tied or were numerically very close, will become your backups, so they won't be wasted. Think of them as your insurance policies, what I call your *extras.* By design, you will have extras at each step so you can pull them back into play if needed.

Recap: Identify, score, and rank your fields of interest following Cara and Sam's templates. You will see that both of them listed ten fields, but you may have more or less. Make the list as long as you want.

Field Template: Cara

Fields That Are Interesting to Me and Why

Health Care: Health care is more important than ever in our world and there are a lot of different ways to go in this field. People look up to people in health care because they are needed and respected for what they do. Success in this field requires you to pay attention to details, which is definitely me.
Q1: 5, Q2: 5, Q3: 5 = Score: 15

Sports/Tennis: Teamwork, having to be all in, and being challenged is what success in sports is all about. Tennis is my thing, and I'm good at it, so anything that I would get paid to do in connection with my sport would be amazing. I also love competition, and this would definitely fit that internal drive.
Q1: 5, Q2: 4.5, Q3: 5 = Score: 14.5

Entertainment: Entertainment would be a nice big umbrella to live under. As an extrovert, I find communication in any form appealing, and combining it with entertainment would be interesting. It's a fast-moving field too, and I'm all for making the most of new opportunities.
Q1: 5, Q2: 5, Q3: 5 = Score: 15

Real Estate: I like real estate because deal making sounds appealing, and there's definitely an element of competition involved. I also feel like real estate would offer a lot of entrepreneurial opportunities, and that could be a really satisfying part of this field.
Q1: 4, Q2: 4, Q3: 5 = Score: 13

Conservation: I care about the planet because I love being outside. When I see people treating the environment in a disrespectful way it totally pisses me off. Going to work every day knowing I was contributing to the planet would be hugely motivational and inspiring.
Q1: 4.5, Q2: 4.5, Q3: 5 = Score: 14

Food: My friends always ask me the best place to go for different kinds of food. It's not as much of a thing for me as tennis, but I love food and finding new restaurants. I also like that food brings people together.
Q1: 4, Q2: 4, Q3: 5 = Score: 13

Consulting: I like figuring out problems and having variety in my work, so consulting is something I've definitely thought about. I also like that it's all about working with other people, which definitely plays to my talents.
Q1: 3.5, Q2: 4, Q3: 4 = Score: 11.5

Music: I love going to music festivals and have definitely sacrificed to be able to afford to go. The feeling it gives you, seeing all kinds of people coming together and just being all about the music, is amazing.
Q1: 5, Q2: 4, Q3: 5 = Score: 14

Technology: There are so many different ways to go here, and I like the idea of working for a start-up. I feel like the opportunity to make money and make a difference, depending on what space you're in, is all up to you. I like a challenge and new territory to cover, so I'm definitely going to look into this field.
Q1: 5, Q2: 5, Q3: 5 = Score: 15

Pets/Animal Advocacy: When my grandma couldn't take care of her dogs anymore, I became the person who cared for them. Knowing I was helping my grandma, but also making sure these two amazing animals were still having a good life, changed me. The idea of a job in which I'm protecting or looking out for animals is definitely appealing.
Q1: 4, Q2: 4.5, Q3: 4.5 = Score: 13

Job Bank: Cara

My Top Five Most Interesting Fields (ranked in order)

1. Entertainment · 2. Health Care · 3. Technology · 4. Sports/Tennis · 5. Music

Field Template: Sam

Fields That Are Interesting to Me and Why

Finance/Money: Money interests me, and I always turn my attention to articles that mention money or investing in the title. It's interesting enough to get a click-through from me.
Q1: 5, Q2: 5, Q3: 5 = Score: 15

Television: I love getting hooked into a storyline and the characters, and binging on what I call really smart TV when I have time.
Q1: 5, Q2: 4.5, Q3: 5 = Score: 14.5

Politics: All in here. I have all the news show apps and check them a lot. Not just US politics but how different governments are run around the globe.
Q1: 5, Q2: 5, Q3: 5 = Score: 15

Snow Sports: My best escape and preferred vacation. When I'm snowboard-ing (preferably) or skiing, I can let everything else go. It gets my attention because it gives me freedom. Plus, I'm competitive and I'm good at it.
Q1: 4.5, Q2: 4, Q3: 4 = Score: 12.5

Law: The law is complex, and using that complexity to win a case or argue a point of view is appealing. Being a good lawyer means research, connecting ideas together, and being persistent. All are very appealing to me.
Q1: 4, Q2: 4, Q3: 4.5 = Score: 12.5

Entrepreneurship: One of my few online subscriptions is to a magazine about entrepreneurs. I love reading and learning about how other people are making money in sometimes obscure ways.
Q1: 4.5, Q2: 4, Q3: 5 = Score: 13.5

Social Media: I like this as a field because it seems to offer a lot of uncharted opportunities in the future. I don't know where it's all going, but it's not going away. Plus, I like the entertainment value it presents and how it rewards creativity.
Q1: 5, Q2: 4.5, Q3: 5 = Score: 14.5

Geology/Astronomy: I love the geology and astronomy courses in my major because I like thinking about how our world was formed and particularly what opportunities for space travel exist. I wouldn't want a job that's all about tracking or identifying objects numerically, but connecting interrelationships and geosystems on a broader level would definitely be interesting to me.
Q1: 4.5, Q2: 4.5, Q3: 5 = Score: 14

Aerospace: My grandfather was an aerospace engineer and I remember going to his house when I was small, looking at the airplane models in his bookcase, and listening to him describe each one. Whenever I see or ride in an airplane, I enjoy thinking about how the physical parts of the plane and navigation systems come together. I do not want to be an engineer, but I would definitely be interested in other types of jobs in this field.
Q1: 4, Q2: 4.5, Q3: 4 = Score: 12.5

Automobiles: I love cars and I spend time on car apps looking at different makes and models. I like the idea of being part of an evolving industry and Elon Musk is a hero of mine. I definitely would be interested in the right job in this field.
Q1: 4.5, Q2: 4, Q3: 4 = Score: 12.5

Job Bank: Sam

My Top Five Most Interesting Fields (ranked in order)

1. Finance/Money · 2. Politics · 3. Social Media · 4. Television · 5. Geology/Astronomy

Check In . . .

This chapter's opening quote by Aristotle, "Pleasure in the job puts perfection in the work," is undeniably true for most people. Thinking of fields as *What's your thing?* is a gateway to putting his good advice into action. As you've just read, focusing on what grabs your attention and what you describe as appealing, fascinating, or stimulating can lead to greater engagement and a deeper connection to your work. This understanding is fundamental to finding a right-fit job, and the stepping stone to creating engagement and connection with a right-fit company, which is where we're headed next. Respect your interest in cars, fashion, real estate, sports, technology—whatever is *your thing*—because it can lead to a job where authentic and sustained intrinsic motivation is a daily reality. And that's exactly what Working *You* is designed to provide.

8

Finding a Right Company

*"Hard work is a prison sentence only
if it does not have meaning."*
—Malcolm Gladwell

Identifying companies that are interesting to you is about being *impressed*. At the company level, you will define what's interesting by being impressed by a company you admire, respect, and trust. Intrinsic motivation requires that you be on the same page as the company. As Malcolm Gladwell states in the opening quote, without meaning, hard work is analogous to a prison sentence. If you have ever worked for a company you didn't admire, respect, and trust, you probably couldn't wait to escape at the end of the day.

Among that small group of happy graduates who love their jobs, admiring, respecting, and trusting the company they work for primarily circled back to three things:

- The Company Deliverable: The key product, service, or business idea the company produces and delivers to the world.
- The Company Culture: The customs and social environment of the company: hierarchical versus flat, diverse and inclusive hiring, open-door management, flexible scheduling, a commitment to having fun at work, and so on.

- The Company Leadership: The investment you believe company leaders are making in your own development with opportunities for you to learn and grow as a professional.

Looking at companies that are interesting to you through the lens of these specific criteria allows you to equip yourself with enough evidence to determine whether or not the company—and you—will be in sync. In addition to believing in the company's main deliverable, being impressed also means that the company's culture represents ideals and principles that you care about. Last, you must trust that the company's leadership will do right by you as an employee by providing you with opportunities to learn and grow professionally. When each of these criteria are met, the job suddenly becomes a lot more about you than about someone else. In this chapter, you will continue to populate your job bank in a way that is personalized for you.

The Why

Simon Sinek, the bestselling British American author whose TED Talk has been watched by tens of millions around the world, has said that "People don't buy what you do, they buy why you do it." As you begin to identify companies at the end of this chapter, set yourself up for a right fit by thinking about working for a company for the "right reasons." For our purposes, the *why* of the company is the total of its primary deliverable, culture, and leadership, as we've discussed. What does that mean? It means that the company's "calling" and how it's achieved resonates and matters to you.

In his renowned TED Talk, Sinek uses the example of the Wright Brothers, the American aviation forerunners recognized for developing, constructing, and also flying the world's first motor-powered airplane. As Sinek points out, Orville and Wilbur were not rich; they owned a bicycle shop. They didn't have government backing or angel investors. But along with a few employees who also shared their same calling, Orville and Wilbur authentically believed in the value of creating a motor-powered airplane. Despite seemingly insurmountable challenges, including numerous crashes over several years, they continued to work at their calling because they believed it *mattered*. The result changed the world forever. History's first motor-powered airplane flight took place on December 17, 1903, in Kill Devil Hills, North Carolina, and was captured in one of the world's most famous photographs.

Because It Makes Me Smile

〜〜〜

Josh Linden is a district manager at Mondelēz International. If that name isn't familiar, perhaps some of its brands are: Oreos, Nabisco, Chips Ahoy, Ritz Crackers, Toblerone, and Cadbury, just to name a few. A multinational US company leading the field of consumer packaged goods (CPG), Mondelēz has approximately 83,000 employees around the world with annual revenue approaching $30 billion.

Josh graduated with an undergraduate degree in business with an emphasis in marketing from California State University, Fullerton. As an undergraduate he completed an internship with Mondelēz, and what impressed him the most about the firm was its culture and stability—two things he admires in a well-run company. He told me that he loves the products the company makes. In fact, during our interview he shared a story about the day he was promoted to district manager.

On that day the company sent a box to his house full of all kinds of new cookies and snack products ahead of their release into the marketplace. "I remember opening up the package, grinning ear to ear, because I knew what was inside. It's the same feeling I remember having when walking down the cookie aisle as a kid. It's why I love getting to experience all of our new products before anyone else through my role at Mondelēz. For me, selling cookies and crackers is without a doubt the fun part of the food industry. I honestly believe in the products we make, and I'm always proud to tell people where I work. It's also a multibillion-dollar international industry, which impresses me too."

Josh's connection to the key products his employer produces shows in his career progression. In just a few short years he's moved up from merchandiser to sales associate, then sales representative, retail merchandising manager, and now district manager, with twelve direct reports and cross-functional management responsibility for a team of almost fifty.

Another thing that impresses Josh is that it's a company that's ethical and team focused. "I don't want to work for a company where I feel like I'm all alone," which speaks directly to both company culture and its leadership. "On Monday morning, I know everyone is behind me." Working for a company with a rich history in the CPG industry also resonated with Josh because of his respect for stability. "When I began my career with Mondelēz, I encountered a number of people who had been with the company for five, ten, fifteen-plus years and had nothing but good things to say about both Mondelēz and the industry. I got a sense early on that this was a company where I could develop and build a long career in the field."

Several years after this first flight, as the Wright Brothers continued to refine and further develop their flying machine, a crash during a test flight severely injured Orville and killed a passenger. A friend who visited Orville in the hospital is documented as having asked him, "Has it got your nerve?" Orville reportedly looked at his friend, slightly puzzled, and repeated, "Nerve? Oh, do you mean will I be afraid to fly again? The only thing I'm afraid of is that I can't get well soon enough to finish those tests next week." That's what believing in the why behind your work is all about, and it's a necessary feature of a right fit between you and the company.

Things to Admire

Each year, *Fortune* magazine generates a top ten list of most admired companies. The companies that regularly seem to land there include Apple, Berkshire Hathaway, Disney, Netflix, and J.P. Morgan. More than 3,500 executives, directors, and analysts worldwide are asked to rank companies in their own fields as to why they admire them, using the nine qualities bulleted below. I'm listing these here because these qualities represent possible criteria you might use when you begin to create your own list of potential companies that impress you.

- Ability to attract and retain talented people
- Quality of management
- Social responsibility to the community and the environment
- Innovativeness
- Quality of products or services
- Wise use of corporate assets
- Financial soundness
- Long-term investment value
- Effectiveness in doing business globally

Another criterion you might consider as you evaluate companies is the F-word—*fun*. I know, work and fun can sometimes sound like completely disparate pursuits. *Can work actually be fun?* You may have heard the exact opposite from people who are grinding away out in the world; they may be hardworking people who simply haven't had the opportunity to combine these two human experiences. I respectfully disagree with anyone who says that work and fun cannot coexist. For those people who love what they do and work with intrinsic motivation each day, work and fun not only coexist, they are intertwined.

Fortune also publishes the annual 100 Best Companies to Work For, which is created by the Great Place to Work Institute. On a year-to-year basis, tens of thousands of employees across all different levels and fields rate their experiences. One of the questions they're asked is whether or not people categorize their company as a fun place to work. Employees who rank their company as "great" also report that it's "fun." As for those companies people rank as "good" rather than "great," far fewer people report that they are also having fun. The farther down a company goes from good to bad, the lower the chance that employees are having fun there. Clearly, there's a positive and negative correlational relationship between these two experiences.

According to the Great Place to Work Institute (its clients include American Express, Deloitte, EY, Hilton, and Salesforce), companies whose employees are happy and having fun experience less turnover. They also produce up to three times the revenue growth and generate much better stock market performance. The bad news across the board in the world of work is that there are overwhelmingly more people not having fun at work— but you already knew that.

So what should you look for in a company's culture to set yourself up to have fun at work? Let me give you a few examples. McGarryBowen, an international ad agency out of New York with clients ranging from Maserati to Disney, offers employees chili cook-offs, Oktoberfest events, Thirsty Thursdays, and a "huge Halloween blowout." On the other side of the country, Symphony, a cloud-based communication and content sharing collaboration platform based in Palo Alto, California, provides employees with a variety of experiences, from massages to margarita machines and monthly outings that include picnics, karaoke, and go-karts. But make no mistake: these companies get a lot of work done and are very serious about their business and products. It goes to what I said about work and fun not only coexisting but being intertwined. Fun is energizing and creates a level of engagement that takes the grind out of work and contributes to productivity and profitability. Be sure to think about the F-word as you begin to list interesting companies that impress you.

Changing How People Think About Beauty

Fatima Ahmed is a marketing manager for Gucci Beauty, a key line of International Coty Luxury, which also includes Bottega Veneta, Burberry, Chloe, Alexander McQueen, and Tiffany & Co. At Gucci, Fatima currently focuses on fragrances, the largest segment of Gucci Beauty, where she's responsible for analyzing trends, examining and understanding market demand, and developing strategies to market the luxury line. She was promoted to manager from assistant manager fairly soon after joining the company. Born and raised in Pakistan, Fatima knew she wanted to step out of her comfort zone for college and experience something new—an early indication of her talent for being adventurous. She thought about college in the UK, but decided to come to the United States because of what she saw as a more "holistic approach to education."

As an undergraduate at USC, Fatima applied for all types of different overseas programs—another clue that she has a talent for being adventurous as well as curious about the world. Following that interest, she took summer internships through university programs in Indonesia, London, and Paris, which gave her a new lens on the world: "These experiences changed me because they opened my eyes to so many different possibilities and perspectives." She likes to challenge herself, and as a result isn't afraid to throw herself into new situations.

The beauty and fashion industries are fields that have always drawn Fatima's attention. One of the things that connects her so firmly to the company she works for is Gucci's mission to change how people think about beauty. "It's not about one look," she told me. "Gucci is showing the world how to challenge conventional thoughts about what's beautiful and inspiring people to express their own beauty in a unique way. This makes me want to get up and go to work, and take our products into the market because I truly believe in this same exact mission. It's my mission too. It definitely makes me feel connected not just to my company, but also to our customers, and that gives me a great sense of being part of something bigger than myself.

"Gucci is changing beauty norms and setting new trends across the world, because they aren't afraid to go up against conformist ideas. Patterns on patterns, for example, was something that you wouldn't do in fashion, and now it's viewed as trendy."

Long before she started to work for the company, she followed it. "I admired Gucci's creative director, Alessandro

Michele, for his unique work and mission to open up the meaning of beauty. When an opportunity came up to work for them, I jumped at it. I'm also a consumer of our products and believe in their value. I love our beauty products, and I am proud to work on such an innovative portfolio. Marketing is exciting for me because of the industry I'm in and the company I work for. I also love that it's competitive, and the combination of the luxury beauty field and marketing is what makes it work for me. It's definitely playing to my interests and strengths."

Working *You*: Identifying Right Companies

Finding a right company requires some research, but I have mapped out the following step-by-step process detailing the most efficient way to go about it.

For each of the top five fields you identified in chapter 7, list all the companies already on your radar that impress you based on everything we've discussed in this chapter.

Then, add to your list by discovering and exploring other companies in these fields. Some of the best resources available include LinkedIn; company information and research sites like D&B Hoovers; job sites like Glassdoor, Indeed, Google for Jobs, Monster, and ZipRecruiter; as well as good old-fashioned Google searches. Here's how to best leverage these types of resources to make them easy to use yet as far-reaching as possible.

LinkedIn: A fast search using your top five fields will get you started. You can narrow your search even further by location. At the company level, we aren't really using LinkedIn to identify networking contacts. The goal is to simply scroll through the list of profiles that pop up when you sort by your five fields to discover companies that might be *interesting*. When you see a company that you want to know more about, make the detour to that company's website and learn more about it right then, while it's fresh in your mind, or do a Google search and see what you turn up. If you uncover information that meets your criteria for being impressed, write it down on your list under its respective field. Or, if you're not impressed, move on.

D&B Hoovers: Many colleges and universities offer students free access to sites like D&B Hoovers through their career centers. If you are still in college, definitely look into which online resources you can access for information about different types of companies in your five fields (or if you have access as an alumnus). Even if you don't have access through your college, there is a free level on Hoovers that will enable you to search for companies. If you're searching by industries—your five identified fields—you will be given a direct link to learn more about any company that sounds like it might be interesting. As I write this book, Hoovers offers a directory of more than eighty-five million companies worldwide, and allows you to sort them all by nine hundred or so different industries. Hoovers also has a handy competitor search function that's very useful. For example, if you find a company you like, you can quickly explore similar companies by clicking on the "competitor" link. What you will then pull up are many more potentially interesting companies that likely weren't on your radar. Write down the names of companies that qualify as interesting. It doesn't matter if you have ten or twenty companies listed for each field—we'll edit the list later.

Online Searches: Entering into your browser search strings such as "Best tech companies to work for in Chicago" or "Best start-ups in Seattle" or "Best small companies to work for in Miami" can lead to some amazing finds. These more targeted searches, incorporating the field, the words "small" or "start-up" or "midsize," and even specific cities or states, will likely turn up companies that you would otherwise not have known about. You may find that you want to have a mix of large companies and start-ups, medium-size companies, and small companies—don't limit yourself if you're open to exploring companies of different sizes. Commit to exploring all of the options that might exist for you and it's quite possible you'll discover a company option that might just qualify as *beyond* interesting. And since you're already there, it's easy to take that important detour and find out more about the company and whether it is indeed worthy of your interest.

Next, rank your companies. Based on a scale of 1 to 5, with 5 once again representing *very interested*, assign three separate numbers (just like you did

Some Research Tips

Dig into each company's product or service, culture, and leadership. *What resonates? What's meaningful to you? What environment sounds fun? What does their mission statement say?* Look up company leaders to see who they are and what they believe in. *Who impresses you? Do you see a shared vision between you and the company? Between you and its leaders?* If the company is large enough to have a philanthropic arm, does this focus have meaning for you? Check out the company's social media presence and see if it resonates. Also, consider what employees have to say about the company. Here, sites like Glassdoor can be very informative. Does it sound like people are having fun? Or is this a company that's going to prevent you from living your best life? Do you see yourself fitting in with what you're finding out about the culture? Are you impressed by what you're discovering? These are all important questions. When you do your research at this personal level, through the lens we've been talking about in this chapter, your job bank will begin to personalize in just the right way, because your answers to all of these questions get to the crux of what's meaningful for *you*. Believe in your value and in the importance of each answer—it's what makes you unique and the system work. Wherever you are in your life, from freshman to senior to graduate school to having already graduated, the process for identifying right-fit companies remains the same. As I mentioned earlier, when we get to Step Three and implementation, we'll use your job bank in a way that makes sense for where you are today.

with fields in the previous chapter) to each company on your list based on your answers to the following three questions:

Q1: Does the company's key product, service, or business idea represent something I believe has value?

Q2: Do the customs and social environment of the company—hierarchical versus flat, diverse and inclusive hiring, open-door management, flexible scheduling, fun, and so on—impress me and are they in sync with my own values?

Q3: Does it appear that company leaders care about the professional development of their employees, and do they represent leadership characteristics that impress me?

Once you're finished scoring each company, total your answers to each of these three questions and then rank them from highest to lowest. Your notes about each company should hold the information you need to assign a score. Your goal is to identify your top five companies within each of your top five fields. The companies that don't rise to the top five will go into your extras list, so don't feel like the detective work you've done is wasted. Remember, you will have extras at each step to tap into later if needed.

Follow Cara and Sam's template examples to see how they used their notes on each company to assign a final score. For the purposes of succinctness, and to keep us moving forward, the following build-outs of right companies in Cara and Sam's templates address only their first three interesting fields. However, at the end of each template, Cara and Sam's updated job banks include their top five companies for all five fields. To see (or download) the full build-outs, check out kirksnyder.com.

Recap: Identify and then score and rank interesting companies in each of your top five fields following Cara and Sam's templates. You may have many more companies listed for each field than you see in the templates, and that's fine. When you have scored and ranked your top five companies in each field, you will now find twenty-five potential right-fit employers in your personalized job bank just like Cara and Sam. You are worth this work! *All of your efforts will pay off when you accept an offer for a job you love.*

Company Template: Cara

Entertainment

ESPN: Would be great to be involved in this field through sports, which I love. Just know about this company because it's something I have always thought about. Categorizing this as entertainment because it's a TV network instead of sports. I like that it's owned by Disney, so there's backing. Indeed and Glassdoor reviews seem good—creative place. Just not sure about staying on East Coast at their HQ, but depends on the job. Could be fun.
Q1: 4.5, Q2: 4, Q3: 4 = Score: 12.5

Netflix: Reed Hastings is an entrepreneur and philanthropist. I like how this company came back and came back big. Love their shows!!
Q1: 5, Q2: 5, Q3: 5 = Score: 15

Hulu: Found using competitor button on Hoovers for Netflix. Forgot about Hulu. Love this too because they are giving power back to viewers and disrupting the cable monopoly. Owned by Disney and NBC Universal.
Q1: 5, Q2: 5, Q3: 4.5 = Score: 14.5

NBC Universal: Lots of ways to go here. Good reviews too—the theme parks could be very interesting in the right role. Never thought about this before. Started thinking about it when I saw they had ownership stake in Hulu along with Disney. Interesting. Lots of roles to explore here.
Q1: 4, Q2: 4, Q3: 4 = Score: 12

YouTube: Searched LinkedIn using entertainment as an industry and saw someone from Haverford working at YouTube. Searched just about YouTube and found the "Originals" department—sounds fun. Didn't know this was there, and it looks like a young energetic group. Also like that they are focusing on music and have their own awards.
Q1: 5, Q2: 4.5, Q3: 4.5 = Score: 14

continued

Virool: Found on The Muse searching "Best New Entertainment Companies to Work For" in Google. I love the word *advertainment*! They're innovative in a thoughtful way, which totally appeals to me. It sounds like they have competitive salaries and are growing.
Q1: 4.5, Q2: 4.5, Q3: 4.5 = Score: 13.5

Sunshine Sachs: PR media focus, found on Observer site after searching "Innovative New Entertainment Companies" in Google—starting to like the PR angle in entertainment—hadn't thought of it before.
Q1: 4.5, Q2: 4.5, Q3: 4.5 = Score: 13.5

Health Care

AbbVie: BioPharm—wasn't thinking about it but sounds interesting—younger company, 2013, plus in Chicago and some good employee reviews—definitely open to going back closer to home. Found searching "Best Health Care Companies in Chicago." Doing Alzheimer's research—maybe an opportunity in that area.
Q1: 4.5, Q2: 5, Q3: 5 = Score: 14.5

Tempus: Same search—in Chicago—merging tech and science—genomic sequencing to cure cancer—employees look younger and diverse—looks like they're having a good time—GOOD perks and benefits.
Q1: 5, Q2: 4.5, Q3: 4.5 = Score: 14

FitBit: I do like San Francisco and love my FitBit—saw on LinkedIn search under Health, Wellness & Fitness Industry with a cross-filter for San Fran just for hell of it. Interesting. Hadn't thought of this before!!! Sort of a cross with tech but putting it here instead.
Q1: 5, Q2: 5, Q3: 5 = Score: 15

GoodRx: Found this randomly on LinkedIn. Love the idea of working for a disrupter when it's a good fight. Making drug prices lower is a mission I could get behind. Making a difference!!! Also, totally fine with moving to L.A.
Q1: 5, Q2: 4.5, Q3: 4.5 = Score: 14

ZappRX: Interesting start-up in Boston. Brings tech into it helping doctors, patients, pharm to manage meds online. Also looks like they work to fast-track new drugs that can save lives—would love working on this "mission."
Q1: 4, Q2: 4, Q3: 4.5 = Score: 12.5

NantHealth: Found this through a Google search "Healthcare Innovation Companies." Really like how they are personalizing health care using a next gen approach to bring the best treatments and people together to deliver health care in a new way. In L.A. too, but also Boston office. Some genome work too—love the future-looking spin on health care—totally exciting to me—creative and making a difference.
Q1: 4.5, Q2: 4, Q3: 4.5 = Score: 13

Technology

Salesforce: I like what they do to help customers manage relationships. I also like Marc Benioff's management style and leadership. Employees say good things about working there. Some alums working there too. Good personality fit.
Q1: 5, Q2: 5, Q3: 5 = Score: 15

Zoom Video: Used this in a class at school and see growth potential. A new level of videoconferencing. If doing tech, why not be in Silicon Valley? Big growth since start-up, impressive. Five stars on Glassdoor from employees, who gets that?! Like the background of Eric Yuan, founder, supersmart.)
Q1: 4.5, Q2: 5, Q3: 5 = Score: 14.5

Expedia: My cousin works for Expedia and has been promoted a couple of times and really likes it! I do like to travel so that would make it more interesting. I found an article online talking about how the leadership of the company is transparent, which is hugely important to me. It seems like a well-organized company and has a lot of potential for growth, which also matters to me.
Q1: 4.5, Q2: 4.5, Q3: 4.5 = Score: 13.5

continued

Intuit: I love that this company is all about taking calculated risks! The Glassdoor reviews seem to cast it as a place where people are themselves, and it has a diverse workforce. It sounds like they really care about their employees. I also checked into their subsidiaries, which sound interesting to me. They are growing, and I like that.
Q1: 4.5, Q2: 5, Q3: 4.5 = Score: 14

Cengage: I like that this is about education but in a new way that's relevant for my generation and for younger kids still in K–12 too. I like the Boston HQ location, which is good for me. What I like most are the articles I found about the leadership; it's *very* visionary and also transparent. They are pretty much leading the way, and I love being part of something new and taking risks.
Q1: 4, Q2: 5, Q3: 5 = Score: 14

LinkedIn: A friend I went to high school with interned there and loved it. I like that it places value on who employees are and making sure they have what they need to succeed. It also sounds fun! They have great food for their employees, wellness programs, and several articles talked about how they are committed to helping their employees grow and be happy. I also like the philanthropy they do—it resonated with me. Also, happy to move to SF area! Keeping my options open!
Q1: 5, Q2: 5, Q3: 5 = Score: 15

Adobe: I use their products and love them. I also turned up that they have a really talented workforce, and that's very appealing. I would be very proud to tell people I worked there. The focus on customers is something I believe in and could see myself contributing to that mission. I like the newer focus on digital marketing, which is definitely an area I would be interested in. San Jose, good weather!!
Q1: 4.5, Q2: 4.5, Q3: 4.5 = Score: 13.5

Updated Job Bank: Cara

(At this point, Cara's updated job bank below reflects the five highest-ranking fields and companies for each of her five identified fields, for a total of twenty-five potential right-fit employers.)

Field: Entertainment
Companies:
- Netflix
- Hulu
- YouTube
- Virool
- Sunshine Sachs

Field: Health Care
Companies:
- FitBit
- AbbVie
- Tempus
- GoodRx
- NantHealth

Field: Technology
Companies:
- Salesforce
- Linked In
- Zoom Video
- Cengage
- Intuit (tie with Cengage)

Field: Sports/Tennis
Companies:
- Wilson
- Nike
- Lululemon
- NCSA
- Turnkey Sports

Field: Music
Companies:
- Shazam
- SoundCloud
- Vevo
- Spotify
- Columbia Records

Company Template: Sam

Finance/Money

New York Life: There seems to be a good commitment to their core values, and I can get behind this. The pay looks good and Business Insider showed a 76 percent high job satisfaction rate among their employees, which is very hopeful. I also like that it sounds like they focus on creating inclusion and support diversity. I feel like there would be a lot of opportunities to create my own path once I was there. Totally open to living in NYC too.
Q1: 4.5, Q2: 4.5, Q3: 4.5 = Score: 13.5

Fannie Mae: I like that the company is headquartered in DC and that they encourage employees to take ten hours of paid time each month for volunteer work through their initiative. This means something to me. There's a fairness element there that resonates. The research I did gave me the sense they are goal driven too. Glassdoor reviews are surprisingly positive, and it's consistently named as a best place to work, winning lots of awards. Looks super-inclusive.
Q1: 5, Q2: 5, Q3: 4.5 = Score: 14.5

Chubb: I have always been interested in working for a company that is European based, and for the finance field Zurich is totally the place to be. High job satisfaction rate for employees—almost 80 percent. It would depend on what kind of roles there are, but I like the idea of working for a company with $20 billion of revenue.
Q1: 4.5, Q2: 4.5, Q3: 5 = Score: 14

Federal Reserve Bank of San Francisco: I like that this Reserve Bank represents twelve districts in the West. It sort of crosses over a lot of fields for me, including politics. I like that it holds the second highest assets after New York, with more than $20 billion in currency notes. I liked studying this in a finance class and thought the whole structure of reserve banks was interesting. It would be great to live in San Francisco. I actually had a professor who started her career there and remember her talking about it positively. Seems super-inclusive and open, but it's still competitive.
Q1: 5, Q2: 5, Q3: 5 = Score: 15

E*Trade: Pay seems to be a bit above some of the other starting pay I've seen, and some of the employee reviews say management encourages free thinking and individuality, which definitely got my attention. Based on my research, the culture seems like it might be a good fit. I have an E*Trade account and have been happy with how it is set up and delivers services. It bridges with tech, which is very interesting to me. It looks like there are some good locations to look at from NYC to Silicon Valley. This is definitely on my list.
Q1: 4.5, Q2: 4.5, Q3: 4 = Score: 13

Loop Capital: I wasn't really thinking about an investment bank because I thought it wouldn't be as innovative, but I want to explore Loop. I really like the combo of being competitive but also diverse and inclusive. I like that it is a full-service investment bank. I actually did talk to the brother of a friend who worked there, and he said it was a good culture and you could succeed based on your hard work. Sounds like it is entrepreneurial, which totally hooks me in!
Q1: 4.5, Q2: 4.5, Q3: 4.5 = Score: 13.5

William Blair: Vault notes that it had "great colleagues and culture" and a no-jerk factor. It also sounds like the pay is somewhat above other employers'. I like that it focuses on the middle market, and it seems that there are a lot of opportunities to grow. Its headquarters are in Chicago, which is totally fine. I actually have some good friends in San Diego who are from Chicago, so that would be helpful. I like what I have read about the CEO, John Ettelson, who seems to have a good commitment to being a civic leader, which I absolutely respect.
Q1: 4.5, Q2: 5, Q3: 5 = Score: 14.5

Politics
Grassroots Analytics: I found this company by googling "new grassroots political consulting firms." It is really shaking up political fund-raising and was founded by a young recent grad from Chapel Hill. It crosses the fields of finance, politics, social media, and technology for me. The more I read about the company, the more excited I got. Love that they are daring to do business in a different way, and would definitely call this company and the people that work there disrupters! So excited about this find!
Q1: 5, Q2: 5, Q3: 5 = Score: 15

continued

Global Strategy Group: I really like that GSG has offices in a lot of cities where I would want to live, including DC, NYC, Chicago, and Denver. The more I learn about Denver the more I like that it is totally on the move, and that's appealing to me. My research on Glassdoor and Vault looks like it is an inclusive company with people who care about what they do. I also like that it has won a lot of awards, and that matters to me because it is a recognized leader in the field. I think I might explore some roles in digital strategy, which would bridge in technology. Denver, here I come? We'll see.
Q1: 4.5, Q2: 5, Q3: 5 = Score: 14.5

Precision Strategies: I read an article about the founder, Stephanie Cutter, and have also watched her as a commentator on TV and was impressed. She's bold, and I see myself as bold and not afraid to go there for something I believe in. I feel like this would be a place where I would get a chance to make a difference and be challenged every day, which is definitely appealing. Would be happy to have the DC experience, but there is also an office in NYC. I also like that they work with clients outside of the US and build the tech infrastructure for driving campaigns. I think this could definitely take advantage of a lot of my talents.
Q1: 5, Q2: 5, Q3: 5 = Score: 15

Elected Congressional Official: I'm putting this down as a company because I feel like there are so many elected officials who would actually serve in the role of a company if you worked for them. I would want to work for a member of Congress instead of the Senate because I feel like it is more on-the-ground and entrepreneurial. I like the strategy part that working for an elected official would require and motivating others to follow me. I also feel like this type of "company" would give me a lot of options to pursue. If this makes it to my job bank of five companies, I will list five members of Congress to focus on. Maybe, we'll see. Low pay though, and if they don't get reelected, you're out. But if they go on to bigger and better things, who knows!
Q1: 4, Q2: 5, Q3: 5 = Score: 14

GMMB: I like that they work with politicians, corporations, and nonprofits. I feel like I would have an opportunity to get behind a lot of different

campaigns and initiatives that I cared about. The company has received many different awards for their work, which I like, and from my research, it looks like I would be able to work across digital and broadcast mediums, which sort of brings into play my interest in the fields of technology and television. I read an interview the founder, Frank Greer, gave, and I really admired how he put different ideas together. This appealed to my out-of-the-box thinking talent! And entrepreneurial side! Seems like there could be a lot of opportunities here.
Q1: 4.5, Q2: 5, Q3: 4.5 = Score: 14

Social Media
Wyng: I really like that this company grew out of Offerpop, which was considered to be one of the world's most popular social marketing platforms. The research I read said that they love smart and hungry hard workers, and that describes me perfectly. I also like that they focus on meeting the personal needs of the clients' customers and helping clients build fast-growing brands on trusted data. This is a big factor for me. Located out of NYC, which works.
Q1: 4.5, Q2: 4.5, Q3: 5 = Score: 14

LYFE Marketing: The reviews on Glassdoor and Vault are pretty impressive. I like that I keep reading about how employees are respected and dedicated. It also looks like there is room to grow, which is a big thing for me. I like that they focus on helping clients grow followers and develop brand awareness, but also about increasing traffic. This definitely appeals to me. The client list is pretty diverse, which I also like. The only thing was I didn't plan on moving to Atlanta, but I am open to exploring.
Q1: 5, Q2: 4.5, Q3: 5 = Score: 14.5

Bread: Great reviews from employees about the culture and opportunities to learn and grow. It looks like a lot of smart people work there, and it's diverse and inclusive. I like that Bread bridges finance and tech. This might blend both fields perfectly, even though I feel like it is more of a tech company. They talk about their mission of bringing dignity to consumer finance, and that's definitely a mission I can get behind. Liking it a lot at this point! And NYC seems to be where all of the action might be for me!
Q1: 5, Q2: 5, Q3: 5 = Score: 15

continued

CrowdTwist: I read about this company when it was purchased by Oracle. I love the entrepreneurial history of CrowdTwist and the analytics platform it uses to let customers interact and provide value with their customers. They have a diverse client list from TOMS to Gatorade to Pepsi and even *The X Factor*, which I like a lot. The purchase by Oracle could mean even greater opportunities, so I am definitely going to explore this company. I also like the focus a lot of employee reviewers talk about, which is innovation.
Q1: 4, Q2: 4.5, Q3: 4 = Score: 12.5

Snapchat: I had to list this because Snap was definitely one of my favorite apps in high school. I like that it keeps changing and updating, which totally appeals to me. I think it can be a lot of things to a lot of people, because the updates allow you to basically tell a story and broadcast it. Some mixed reviews from employees, but I am going to look at roles here and explore more to figure it out for myself. Some might not like it, but I might love it. To me, it sounds like a fun place to work, and I love that it has such a huge audience. I feel like I would be maximizing my impact. Also, it's based in L.A., which just might be the best! Lots of friends from SDSU in L.A.
Q1: 5, Q2: 4, Q3: 5 = Score: 14

FUEL Marketing: I hadn't thought that much about Boston, but a friend of mine from school who graduated last year told me about FUEL, and then I did more research for my job bank and liked what I saw. They are providing clients with communication strategy, and seem to be really forward-thinking and innovative to help their clients solve business problems. I was impressed that almost 90 percent of their business comes from referrals. It seems like there might be an opportunity to explore some analytics too, like traffic rates, social media numbers, and retention rates. And I like that it's a start-up and entrepreneurial.
Q1: 4.5, Q2: 4.5, Q3: 4 = Score: 13

Updated Job Bank: Sam

(Just like Cara, at this point Sam's updated job bank reflects the five highest-ranking fields and five highest-ranking companies for each field for a total of twenty-five potential right-fit employers.)

Field: Finance/Money
Companies:
- Federal Reserve Bank of
- San Francisco
- Fannie Mae (tie with William Blair)
- William Blair
- Chubb
- Loop Capital

Field: Politics
Companies:
- Precision Strategies (tie with Grassroots Analytics)
- Grassroots Analytics
- Global Strategy Group
- Elected Congressional Official GMMB

Field: Social Media
Companies:
- Bread
- LYFE Marketing
- Wyng (tie with Snapchat)
- Snapchat
- CrowdTwist

Field: Television
Companies:
- Hulu
- NBC Universal
- Apple
- YouTube
- MSNBC

Field: Geology/Astronomy
Companies:
- SpaceX
- National Park Service
- Blue Origin
- Virgin Orbit
- NASA

Check In . . .

Finding companies that impress you because of their mission, company culture, and leadership—or because, like Josh Linden, their product makes you smile—will create the meaning you're seeking. Identifying interesting companies that you admire, respect, and trust will contribute to making your job a place you want to break *into* rather than *out of.* Your job bank is expanding and you've hit the twenty-five goal for potential right-fit employers. My best advice is to make sure you fully explore and research all companies that might qualify as interesting to you in each of your identified fields. This effort will make the next part of building your custom job bank—adding specific roles—as *meaningful* as it can be. You deserve a job that's in a right field, a right company, and a right role—one that's perfect for you.

9

Finding a Right Role

"Hide not your talents. They for use were made.
What's a sundial in the shade?"
—Benjamin Franklin

Identifying roles that are interesting to you and attaching yourself to a job title means you need to ask yourself two important questions:

1. What sounds authentically enjoyable?
2. Where will my Functional Value be leveraged most?

Aside from enjoying a fun work environment based on amazing perks, authentically enjoying what you do each day plays a key role in creating the right connection between who you are and what you do. If a role doesn't sound enjoyable, there's a good reason for that, and it's not the job for you.

Once a potential role has passed the test of the first question, which has relevancy across both your Human Value and Image Value, the second question is about finding a role that rewards you for your Functional Value, which of course represents your talents and skills. Think about this chapter's opening quote from Benjamin Franklin for a moment. What good are your talents and skills if you don't put them to use in a place where they can work *for you*? Those happy new graduates who love their job are always leveraging their talents and skills, which is why they authentically enjoy performing their work. Their Functional Value is strongly rewarded because their job takes advantage of their talents, which captures and keeps their attention. For those who hate their job, it's the opposite. For most people, struggling to perform in any context when you're not particularly good at what you're doing, isn't very enjoyable—and it's particularly not enjoyable when it's your job and you have to perform at a certain level or get fired. Remember, *the wind at your back*.

Leveraging Your Talents as Natural Strengths

Adam Bryant of the *New York Times* writes a highly popular weekly series on management and leadership called Corner Office. In a column titled "How to Hire the Right Person," Bryant presented findings based on interviews with nearly five hundred business leaders. It seems that making a right hire had little to do with someone's college major or current job title, and everything to do with what he terms "natural strengths." On this subject, Bryant defines a right hire based on being able to effectively apply an ability that comes as "naturally as breathing," but is nonetheless an ability that others find difficult. I want you to think about that for a moment, It speaks directly to what you have defined as your own unique talents and why it's so critical to write with your correct hand when it comes to finding work you love. *It's the recipe for leveraging your natural strengths.*

When working with students to identify right roles, I often start by asking them to consider how they go about picking an elective class. It's no surprise that most students are attracted to courses that sound enjoyable because there is a *talent connection* to the deliverables of the course. Unfortunately, some students ignore this connection and take an elective they really don't want to take because they believe it will bolster their resume. While there is arguably some merit (sometimes) to that line of thinking, when it comes to identifying right-fit roles, don't even consider pursuing a role just for the sake of your resume's bullet points. Identify roles you believe represent a match between your Functional Value (with a specific focus on your talents) and what the job functionally requires to be a successful performer.

Discovering What's Interesting to You

Susan Wojciki is the current CEO of YouTube. Back in 1998 she famously rented garage space to Larry Page and Sergey Brin, the founders of Google, as they began a start-up that evolved into one of the largest and most successful culture-changing technology companies in the world. Majoring in history and literature and coming from a highly accomplished academic family, Wojciki's original plan for a career in academia changed when she discovered something that was interesting *to her*. Wojciki has attributed a computer science course she took in college as having changed how she thinks.

Joining Google as its sixteenth employee (there are nearly one hundred thousand now), her role at the company made a tremendous and undeniable impact on Google's global success. From developing AdWords, a game-changing system in which advertisers bid on specific keywords as a vehicle for their ads to appear in Google's search results, to pioneering content-sharing through Google Video, to recommending and managing the purchase of YouTube, it's safe to say that Wojciki leveraged her talents as natural strengths in each of her evolving and highly impactful roles. In a *Time* magazine profile, Academy Award–winning producer Brian Grazer said about Wojciki, "She has this innate navigational system that enables her to operate on a higher plane." As a problem solver, Wojciki herself has stated, "If you come into a company and see something is not working, fix it." But being a problem solver also requires the ability to *listen*, which is itself a talent that can also be described as empathy. In fact, you might have identified listening or empathy as your talents earlier in the book. I thought it was noteworthy that in another interview, Wojciki actually said about her own leadership roles, "As you get more senior, your job is to hear what's not working so you can make it better." I think it's safe to say that listening could be identified as one of the natural strengths she has applied in her career.

Now, specific to what Grazer described in the *Time* profile as Wojciki's "innate navigational system," I also think it's safe to say that having a talent for intuition can assist in making good business decisions. When asked about her decision to join Page and Brin at Google, which at the time meant leaving a secure job at Intel, Wojciki declared, "It didn't seem like a risky decision. I saw that this is the future."

Finding a Right Role

One year after graduating from Binghamton University, one of four university centers in the State University of New York (SUNY) system, Ashley Hilfman is more certain than ever that she found her own right role as a People's Advisory Services consultant at Ernst & Young.

Working in the career center while an undergraduate at Binghamton, she had a bird's-eye view of many different companies and "who" they are. Ashley began working in the career center as part of a student work program in order to pay for books and dues for student organizations she knew she needed to join. Binghamton has a wonderful program that promotes academic success and personal growth for first-generation college students, income-eligible students, and students with disabilities. Through innovative practices and programming, eligible students are better able to achieve their academic and professional goals while at the same time enriching their overall college experience. Coming from what she describes as a low-income background, Ashley told me, "The program opened doors for me and helped me believe in myself and my goals and dreams."

Ashley is one of those rare students who graduated from Binghamton with a degree in business administration with three areas of emphasis. "In the business school, you can major in business administration and then create an emphasis based around whatever interests you most. I completed one emphasis in leadership and consulting because I had been exposed to this path working at the career center. I knew I had a connection to this role. I had the right talents and I was good at it. It made sense to me."

Anytime I meet someone who is driven to go so far beyond what was expected of them, I immediately want to know more. When I asked Ashley what drove her to graduate with three areas of emphasis, she responded, "I wanted to maximize my skill set anywhere I found that I had a natural strength or an interest." She chuckled as she shared, "I guess you can tell I'm interested in a lot! But that's just who I am—I guess you could call it being curious."

Her experience of identifying a right company before finding a right role serves as a great model. Ashley started thinking about consulting, and, in particular, working at Ernst & Young, after attending a business panel. "It was a Women in Business panel, and being able to see so many high-performing and successful women talk specifically about inclusive environments was inspiring. After the event, the women from E&Y stayed and talked to the students long after the event was over. That really impressed me. From there, I started looking for E&Y at other events, and each time, the behavior of the recruiters backed up the talk. That's when I started to know this company was the one I wanted to join."

Ashley compared this panel to a not-so-great experience she had at another conference designed for students who were part of the same student support program she had joined at Binghamton. When she went up to talk to one of the speakers and express interest in the company, she was told that she wouldn't get a job there because Binghamton wasn't one of their target recruiting schools. "I wondered, why did you invite us here to tell us how great your company is, and then basically tell me I wasn't good enough to work there? That was all I needed to know, and it actually motivated me to work even

harder. I knew I only wanted to work for a company that walked the talk. Otherwise, it's all just for show. For any student who has been told that they're not good enough because of their background or school, don't accept it. It just means that particular company isn't worthy of your time. Go to a company that will believe in you. You can do whatever you want to do if it's right for you."

Because Ashley did the work and found a right-fit field and company, the role she then identified to fully leverage her Functional Value was the last fit point she needed to lock in her job. When I talk to Ashley, I can hear the authentic enjoyment she finds through her work. Remember, there's a connection between that kind of authentic enjoyment and being able to leverage one's Functional Value in a role. Recognizing that connection will help you use your right fields and companies to find the right role.

Wojciki has clearly applied her talents and skills to each of her roles as she successfully progressed through her career. You have the same opportunity to apply *your* natural strengths in your first role out of college, and in each role after that, so that your functional job performance comes as "naturally as breathing." This chapter will equip you with the necessary insight to figure out how to connect your own natural strengths—your talents as you've defined them through your Functional Value point—to the Success Factors of a right-fit role in each of the twenty-five companies that are now sitting in your personal job bank.

Getting More Focused

To zero in on your own right roles, it's time to get more focused. Begin by summarizing your talents to serve as a guide as you begin to identify right-fit roles. Go back to LinkedIn, but this time wear a different set of glasses. Using the twenty-five potential employers that are now in your job bank, enter each company name into LinkedIn's search field and look at the job titles listed in the employee profiles, keeping in mind your own talents.

As you zero in on specific roles that sound interesting, pay attention to your spontaneous reactions to the descriptions. For example, if the role requires you to provide a monthly financial analysis of all new product lines, does that sound enjoyable or perhaps even motivating? Or does it sound like punishment? There is a reason you have positive or negative reactions to the thought of performing specific roles, and these reactions definitely have relevance when it comes to identifying a right fit.

For any job title that creates a positive spontaneous reaction, dig deeper and explore what that specific role is all about. You may find that someone has listed resume-type entries within their LinkedIn profile. Carefully look at what the role would call on you to do as you consider your own fit. If the role still looks interesting, jump out of LinkedIn while it's fresh in your mind and go to the company's website. Look under "careers" or "jobs" or whatever designation is used to categorize employment opportunities. See if that job is listed in order to learn more about what the employer was originally looking for when that opening was posted. While you're on the company's site, look through the other job listings with the same mind-set: Is there another similar role that would leverage your Functional Value? Finally, do an online search using the specific job title and company. I've seen students find original job listings that were not on the company's site but were cached somewhere in the cobwebs of the internet. This allows you to uncover more specific information about what that employer was looking for in a successful candidate for that exact role.

Do your best to focus only on those roles you will be qualified for as a new or recent graduate, whether that's now, next semester, next year, or two years from now. This is an important point. I don't want you to waste your time pursuing jobs that you won't be hired for because they are beyond the reasonable qualifications of a new or recent college graduate. However, if you do see a more advanced position that sounds fun and you believe it's within a functional area or department that's appealing and would play to your natural strengths, give yourself the challenge of finding out if there is a more appropriate-level role in that same department that you *would* be qualified for when you apply for the job.

If you find five roles in one company, write them all down. You will narrow the list to just one role per company later. If there's only one role, there's only one. If you don't find any roles, that's okay too. Go back to your extras list and pull your next-highest-ranking company for that field into play. And if you find you need more fields, go back to your extras list for fields. Your insurance policies are there for you to draw on. The goal is to always keep twenty-five companies represented in your job bank so you end up with a full menu of twenty-five right-fit jobs to pursue.

In addition to LinkedIn and the company's website, visit other job listing sites like Indeed, Glassdoor, Google for Jobs, Monster, ZipRecruiter, or your preferred resource. Immediately drill down to the companies on your list and see what roles you find. I also encourage you to enter the company's name into your browser along with any functional area and the word *jobs*. A functional area, for example, might be marketing, human resources, communication, or finance. For example, you might search "Electronic Arts, Programming, Jobs" to see what turns up. I just did, and was linked to sixty-five potential programming roles at Electronic Arts to explore through a wide variety of linked sites.

Working *You*: Identifying Right Roles

Once you've collected all of this highly targeted intelligence on roles, it's time to pick what you believe is the most interesting role at each company. Again, for some companies you may have only one role listed, and that's fine. You're done. For those companies where you listed more than one role, now you'll select your *preferred* role for that company to enter into your job bank.

To do this, focus on your talents (the wind at your back) when it comes to functionally performing the role. Assign a score of 1 to 10 to how strongly you believe the role will leverage your talents as natural strengths. (I use a 1 to 10 scale at the role level to allow for more nuance between similar roles.) Look closely at what the listing from the employer states about the job itself and the abilities of the preferred candidate as well as the resume of anyone who currently is or has been employed in the role. If the scores are the same or too close to rank, go back to what we've called the *F-word*. Which company sounds more *fun*? Save the other roles for your extras list; you can pull them from your back pocket if you need them later on. For example, if the role you choose isn't available at the time you are applying for jobs, pulling into play a tie or another role that scored high is why the extras list exists. Weighing more than one right role at the same company is a good problem to have.

As you can see in Cara and Sam's template examples, the goal is to leave this chapter with one identified role for each of your twenty-five companies, along with a set of notes about what you discovered as you collected your intel for each role. Your notes should focus on why you believe the role would be authentically enjoyable and would leverage and reward your Functional Value focusing specifically on your talents.

For the purposes of illustration, following are completed build-outs of roles in Cara and Sam's first two fields, along with fully updated job banks at the end of the template reflecting their highest-ranked roles in all twenty-five companies. If you would like to see Cara and Sam's build-outs for all five fields, they are available to view or download at kirksnyder.com.

Recap: Remind yourself of the value of your talents and explore roles at each company in your job bank. List all of the roles that sound authentically enjoyable and will reward your Functional Value (with a big focus on leveraging your talents). Following the example of Cara and Sam's templates, score and rank each of your twenty-five roles to identify the top right role for each company.

Role Template: Cara

Note: Job titles and descriptions are not intended to represent available jobs at any of the companies listed here; they are for illustrative purposes only.

Collective Talents

Competitive. Determined. Outgoing. Social. Athletic. Agile. Detail-oriented. Astute. Tactical. Communicator. Clever. Focused. Vigilant. Logical problem solver. Motivated. Involved. Calculated risk taker.

Top Five Talents

Detail-oriented. Competitive. Logical problem solver. Communicator. Involved.

Entertainment Companies

Netflix

Roles:

- Coordinator, Leadership Programs: Create and design nontraditional and experiential events to allow top leaders to explore leadership values and development. About fostering great leaders and great human beings. Want someone detailed who can communicate but also create a vision. Ranking: 9
- Social Media Assistant Manager, Employer Branding: Focuses on creating branding efforts at Netflix all over the world. Taking the Netflix brand and bringing it to life on social media. Want someone strategic and analytical, collaborative and resourceful—that's me! Ranking: 10

Hulu

Roles:

- Associate, Originals Marketing and Social: Part of a team that works to drive interest, viewing, and engagement for series and films. Looking for someone who has the right balance of strategic acumen and communication skills and knowledge of social media. Ranking: 10

continued

YouTube

Roles:

- Social and Influencer Marketing, Coordinator: This group works on how social media are integrated into all touch points, from ad campaigns to marketing and customer service. Collaborate across different marketing departments at YouTube to align efforts and create social media strategies. Looking for someone who is focused and detail-oriented but with strong communication skills and can bring things together in unconventional ways. Ranking: 9

- Coordinator, Creative Partnerships: Works on team that focuses on the global strategy and partner management for YouTube's biggest creators and public figures. Looking for someone who can help develop and implement strategies for stakeholders cross-functionally within the company. Want someone that has excellent communication skills, can solve problems, and can connect the dots on their own. Ranking: 10

Virool

Roles:

- Business Development Manager: Focus on all facets of building external relationships. Find acquisition or investment opportunities and negotiate partnerships. Looking for someone who is a fast learner, can build strong rapport with partners, and is intellectually curious. Ranking: 9.5

Sunshine Sachs

Roles:

- Junior Account Executive, Talent and Influencer: Looking for someone who can develop trusting relationships quickly. Assist in developing and executing comprehensive communication strategies. Schedule and provide logistical support for meetings. Work with senior management to respond to client requests. Ranking: 9

- Social Media Analyst: Need good analytical skills, be detail-focused. Translate key findings into easy-to-understand language and present them to clients. Conduct research on various social media topics and communicate it to senior managers. Looking for someone with strong decision-making abilities and accountability. Ranking: 9.5

Health Care Companies

FitBit

Roles:
- Assistant Product Manager: Defining mobile software products that impact the health of millions of users. Participate in setting product strategy and work closely with engineering, design, marketing, and leadership. Looking for someone to develop and communicate product priorities, collaborate with multiple teams, and be self-motivated and self-directed. Ranking: 9
- Research Coordinator: Identify and recruit participants for a variety of research studies based on design and needs—figuring out what customers want and why. Identify and manage research vendors and resources. Looking for someone with exceptional organizational skills, self-starter, and interest in and passion for people and cultures. Ranking: 9.5

AbbVie

Roles:
- Instructional Designer: Assist in coordination of activities of a cross-functional team to ensure that development of necessary training solutions are completed on time and on budget. Lead projects with planning and implementation, including developing course descriptions and training materials. Need good communication skills and someone who can solve problems and handle challenges. Ranking: 9.5

continued

Tempus

Roles:

- Junior Sales Account Executive: Responsible for building and maintaining relationships with doctors and office staff to drive orders. Coordinate medical affairs report reviews with doctors and convey clinical data and progress notes for patients to all accounts. Attend conferences and represent company. Looking for a quick learner, ability to maintain and organize a high level of market customer and product knowledge, positive attitude, and an outgoing personality with strong communication skills. Hadn't thought a lot about sales, but it fits and can take me to other roles in health care. Ranking: 9.5

- Partner Operations Coordinator: This is about supporting the sales team and also working with the clinical side. Focused specifically on cancer genomics, which is really appealing—it's bold and breaking new ground. It focuses on managing data to work with cross-functional teams to redefine how genomic data is used in real-world settings. Need someone highly organized and systematic with great attention to detail. They also noted "persistent" on the job description, which is totally me. Yes!!! Ranking: 10

GoodRx

Roles:

- Compliance Associate: Responsible for coordinating marketing initiatives across online and offline marketing teams to ensure marketing materials are in compliance with legal and regulatory agencies. Works with legal team, marketing teams, and senior leadership to educate, collaborate with, and make recommendations to be sure all marketing is compliant. Need someone who is highly organized, with exceptional attention to detail. This is interesting to me because I have thought about law school in the future, and this could lead to it. Sounds boring to my friends, but I actually think it sounds fun. Ranking: 9

NantHealth

Roles:

- Product Management Associate: Work with client implementation team to help deliver projects to clients across all product lines. Action-oriented and pragmatic. Work in a collaborative environment with analysts, engineers, and stakeholders at client organizations to implement client projects. In a way, this is an in-house consultant solving problems and communicating in a transparent way. Looking for someone who is logical, outgoing, and detail-oriented. Ranking: 9

- Client Support Analyst: Responsible for providing direct support to customers and end users to address client needs. Requires someone who is motivated, detail- and goal-oriented, and can multitask. Need someone who can identify trends, effectively communicate with and report trends to leadership, and not be afraid of complex problems. Need to be vigilant and driven. Ranking: 10

Updated Job Bank: Cara

At this point, Cara has identified a role for each of her twenty-five companies and is ready to move forward to rating and ranking them in the next chapter.

Field: Entertainment
Companies and Roles:
- Netflix: Social Media Assistant Manager, Employer Branding
- Hulu: Associate, Originals Marketing and Social
- YouTube: Coordinator, Creative Partnerships
- Virool: Business Development Manager
- Sunshine Sachs: Social Media Analyst

Field: Health Care
Companies and Roles:
- FitBit: Research Coordinator
- AbbVie: Instructional Designer
- Tempus: Partner Operations Coordinator
- GoodRx: Compliance Associate
- NantHealth: Client Support Analyst

Field: Technology
Companies and Roles:
- Salesforce: Sales Apprentice
- LinkedIn: Business Leadership Program Associate
- Zoom Video: Customer Marketing Campaign Associate
- Cengage: Marketing Coordinator
- Intuit (tie with Cengage): Associate Marketing Manager, Social Media & Advertising

Field: Sports/Tennis
Companies and Roles:
- Wilson: Channel Management Specialist
- Nike: Global Membership and Consumer Knowledge Program
- Lululemon: Associate, Product Management
- NCSA: Recruiting Coordinator
- Turnkey Sports: Marketing Manager

Field: Music
Companies and Roles:
- Shazam: Account Executive
- SoundCloud: Artist Relations
- Vevo: Optimization Specialist
- Spotify: Client Solutions
- Columbia Records: Marketing Assistant

Role Template: Sam

Collective Talents
Goal-driven. Dedicated. Strategic. Independent. Creative. Big-picture thinker. Inventive. Brave. Nonconformist. Inspired. Determined. Curious.

Top Five Talents
Creative. Inspired. Determined. Dedicated. Curious.

Finance/Money Companies

Federal Reserve Bank of San Francisco

Roles:
- Research Analyst: Looking for solid analytical and decision-making abilities and good communication skills. Assist economists in analyzing public policy issues and events. Need some experience with databases, which might not be perfect right now, but I can still take an elective class to develop these skills before graduation. Plan and execute long-term research with economists, which sounds like it would take advantage of some of my talents, but need to talk to someone there to learn more about what it's really like. Ranking: 8

Fannie Mae

Roles:
- Quality Control Specialist: Provide oversight on loan quality and compliance. Consult on best practices. Develop, implement, and recommend credit standards. Research frauds and patterns, which sounds interesting. Doesn't sound like it would allow me to be creative or think at a global level. Sounds pretty structured. If I need to, I could definitely swap out this company at the end. Ranking: 5

William Blair

Roles:

- Analyst: Lots of opportunities to work in specific groups like technology, equity capital markets, or consumer and retail. Love this scope! Technology sounds perfect. Immediate client contact and global mobility plus ongoing opportunities for training, which I also love the sound of! Gain understanding of client investment styles and needs, and suggest methods for positioning WB's advantages over its competitors—love the sound of this! Totally plays into my competitiveness. Also need you to offer creative and insightful resolution to issues that arise in execution and origination. Ranking: 10

- Research Associate: Develop knowledge of assigned industry and companies and keep up on all new market developments. Analyze research to identify trends and also review financial information related to the sector. Looking for someone to work independently and also support team goals. Ranking: 9

Chubb

Roles:

- Finance Analyst Associate: Need someone to work closely with various finance units on a variety of projects and processes, including other analysts as well as company leaders. Analyze data, improve financial status by recommending changes based on statistical reports, reconcile transactions. Might not be creative enough for me, and not sure my talents will support my performance. If I need to, I could definitely swap out this company at the end too. Ranking: 6

continued

Loop Capital

Roles:

- Investment Analyst: Support leaders on all aspects of business development and deal acquisition. Assist state and local governments to access capital markets; this would pull politics into play a little bit. Serve as a project manager, create and review debt profiles for target clients, alert team to new opportunities. Need someone who has a strong work ethic, that's definitely me. Also, someone who is self-motivated and confident—also me. Ideal candidate is driven and dedicated. Ranking: 9.5

Politics Companies

Precision Strategies

Roles:

- Mobilization and Campaign Associate: Looking for someone to support and drive the campaign strategies including mobilizing grassroots and building organizations from the ground up. Want someone dedicated and strategic who can understand data analytics. Need to develop a creative vision and strategy for clients. Ranking: 9

Grassroots Analytics

Roles:

- Operations Associate: Perform donor and candidate research, leverage technology to help candidates target voters and donors, assist in developing database. Assist with business development and outreach, analyze trends, and create new media opportunities to serve clients. Ranking: 9

Global Strategy Group

Roles:

- Communication and Public Affairs Practice Associate: Ideal candidates have creativity and are committed to meeting important deadlines. Build coalitions on digital and social media campaigns. Looking for candidates who can work in a fast-paced environment and who are motivated, responsible, and proactive—that's me. Assist senior team in development and execution of campaign plans, including grassroots/field and digital engagements. Looking for a natural problem solver who is strategic and wants to work hard. Ranking: 10

Elected Congressional Official

Roles:

- Congressional Aide: Support elected official in whatever duties are required, from research to handling e-mails. Attend meetings with congress member, sometimes manage calendars, and just be ready to go with whatever is happening day by day. You can work in DC or at the local state office, so there are different ways to go. Definite opportunities to grow if you are dedicated, which I am. You can make an impact depending on your initiative. I want to network with two alums from SDSU that I see on LinkedIn are working on the Hill to find out more. It could be an exciting option and definitely bold, which I like a lot. Ranking: 9.5

GMMB

Roles:

- Assistant Account Executive: Assist teams on projects, including conducting research, updating status reports, and coordinating logistics between different departments. Looking for someone with strong attention to detail who can distill and streamline information. Need to be flexible and available when clients need you. Create and drive advocacy campaigns that deliver real results. Might be more logistics in terms of administrative support that could work against me, but I'm leaving it on my list to talk to someone who is inside, because I really resonate with the company. Ranking: 8

Updated Job Bank: Sam

Like Cara, at this point, Sam has also identified a role for each of his twenty-five companies and is ready to rank them.

Field: Finance/Money
Companies and Roles:
- William Blair: Analyst
- Loop Capital: Investment Analyst
- William Blair: Research Associate
- Federal Reserve Bank: Research Analyst
- Chubb: Finance Analyst Associate

Note: Because Sam had more than one role listed for some companies in his job bank, you will notice that there are two roles listed for the William Blair company. This is fine. The goal here is to list your top-five-ranked roles even if that means having two different roles at the same company.

Field: Politics
Companies and Roles:
- Global Strategy Group: Communication and Public Affairs Practice Associate
- Elected Congressional Official: Congressional Aide
- Grassroots Analytics: Operations Associate
- Precision Strategies: Mobilization and Campaign Associate
- GMMB: Assistant Account Executive

Field: Social Media
Companies and Roles:
- Bread: Product Analyst
- LYFE Marketing: Social Media Specialist
- Wyng (tie with Snapchat): Assistant Project Manager
- Snapchat: Product Communications Specialist
- CrowdTwist: Assistant Manager, Client Success

Field: Television
Companies and Roles:
- Hulu: Marketing Strategy Associate
- NBC Universal: Associate, Corporate Strategy and Development
- Apple: Content Strategy and Optimization Apple TV+
- YouTube: Development Associate, YouTube Originals
- MSNBC: Digital Operations Coordinator

Field: Geology/Astronomy
Companies and Roles:
- SpaceX: Market Analysis Associate
- National Park Service: Data Analyst
- Blue Origin: Operations Strategist
- Virgin Orbit: Associate, Government Affairs
- NASA: Public Affairs Specialist

Check In . . .

Enjoyment is something we experience when we're having a good time. It's the by-product of engaging in an activity that creates pleasure. Authentically enjoying your work because it rewards who you are while pointing you toward your own definition of success is what a right role in a right field and company will generate. Part of the enjoyment equation is most definitely having the opportunity to engage your talents to successfully perform your job. As Benjamin Franklin advised in this chapter's opening quote, do not hide your talents. He is telling us that our unique talents were made to be used. A sundial in the shade? It's perfectly useless. A sundial in the sun? It's perfectly astonishing. That's exactly what a right-fit job will do for you in your career . . . *facilitate astonishing.*

As we finish Step Two in the Working *You* system and begin to create your own blueprint to find a job you love in Step Three, take time to appreciate the hard work you have already put into your future. Reflect on all that you bring to the job market and your potential to be *astonishing* when your job is in the sun. *Now it's time to get some sunlight.*

STEP THREE

Implementation and Getting Your Perfect Job

"Let our advance worrying become advance thinking and planning."
—Winston Churchill

To finalize your job bank and put it into action, you'll use a custom blueprint based on your own unique *timeline*. For example, if you will be graduating within one year (for undergraduate and graduate students alike) or you have already graduated, you're ready to begin turning your right-fit jobs into offers *now* (like Sam). If you have a year or more to go until graduation (like Cara), you will use your blueprint as a tool to maximize the time between now and that one-year countdown in order to become as competitive a candidate as possible. Then, when the time is right, you will be completely ready to turn your right-fit jobs into offers. This might mean pursuing internships or part-time or summer jobs in your identified right-fit companies and converting them into full-time employment offers later on. Or it might mean leveraging your talents to build skills that create an even stronger connection between your Functional Value and the Success Factors of a right-fit job by targeting relevant elective classes or taking on leadership roles in student or community organizations. Your blueprint will have a simple recalibration built in to incorporate new personal and professional experiences along with any changes in the external marketplace. When you are ready to pursue offers, this ensures that your blueprint is always completely up to date. I've tested multiple student timelines and found that freshman and sophomore students who build out their plans well in advance of graduation gain a heightened sense of direction and self-awareness that ultimately sets them apart from their peers. It also reduces stress—and that is a very good thing.

In the next two chapters, I'll discuss different timeline scenarios and provide guidance to fully build out and implement your own Working *You* blueprint. At the end of this final section of the book, I'll talk about how to use the system in years to come to manage your career so you'll always be fueled by intrinsic motivation in work you love. But for now, regardless of your class standing, it's time to put the finishing touches on your personal job bank before putting together your blueprint to turn right fits into offers. Let's make your future happen!

Don't Stay Stuck

If at any point you find yourself in a job that's not a fit, don't worry. You're not alone, and you're not stuck. As I mentioned earlier in the book, studies have indicated that two out of ten new graduates have a job that requires a degree, but it's a job they hate. If you are a recent graduate or new professional and identify with this experience, use the following implementation section to get out of a bad fit and into a right fit. Unless the job is taking a mental or physical toll and compromising your well-being or you feel unsafe, try to stick it out until you have an offer for a new right-fit job. What I've found is that people gain a sense of empowerment when they begin to build a map out of that bad fit that somehow makes the time remaining more palatable. There's no valor in staying in a job you hate any longer than it takes to find a job you love. *You deserve work you love.*

10

You and the Job: Is It a Fit?

"The shoe that fits one person pinches another."
—Carl Jung

I love this opening quote from Carl Jung because what you're doing in this chapter is essentially measuring the fit of all twenty-five jobs in your job bank. It's all about making sure the job doesn't *pinch* before you go for it. Since Jung's work is also the foundation of the MBTI personality assessment you saw in chapter 2, I thought these were definitely *fitting* words. As you measure the strength of each job to find your best right fits, you will have all of the necessary information at the end of this chapter to then build your custom blueprint in the next and final chapter.

To get there, first you'll rank the twenty-five jobs listed in your job bank based on the strength of the fit between your You Points and the Employer Points for each job. Then, you will further prioritize them into your top ten *best* right fits. You will also apply one last real-world layer of information to confirm that your best right fits are on point, and recalibrate, if necessary, by pulling your extras (jobs ranked eleven to twenty-five) into play. Once you've finalized and vetted the ranking, we will work together in the book's final chapter to create the blueprint that will turn your right fits into job offers along *your* unique timeline.

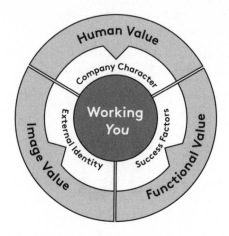

You will approach this in two steps: 1) Score the strength of the Working *You* fit for each job in your job bank and 2) collect an important final layer of accuracy about what each job is really like with real-world information from people working in these environments to make sure you have scored the strength of the fit accurately. Again, it's about trying these jobs on as best you can to make sure they don't pinch before buying them.

Scoring the Strength of the Fit

The best way to approach the first step is to rank each job in your job bank right now by assessing the strength of the fit at each of the three Working *You* fit points. Based on all the information you've gathered on your own, which is substantial, simply assign a numerical score from 1 to 5 (with 5 being the highest) to rate the fit between each of your You Points and the correlating Employer Points of each job. For example, for any given job in your job bank, you might rate the strength of the fit between your Human Value and the employer's Company Character as 5, between your Functional Value and the employer's Success Factors as 4, and between your Image Value and the employer's External Identity as 5. In this case, that particular job has an overall score of 5 + 4 + 5 = 14 out of a possible 15. Each job in your job bank will therefore have a separate number assigned to each fit point along with a final score. You will see these scores represented in Cara and Sam's templates at the end of this chapter.

The second part is simply about zeroing in on your top ten highest-scoring fits. By separating out your best right fits, adding in the final layer of real-world information becomes much more manageable and focused. And if that final layer of real-world information proves that your scoring of each fit point wasn't completely accurate, it's not a problem. Revise the score and recalibrate your list—just like an Excel sheet. If one job drops out of the top ten, the next-highest-scoring job will be pulled *into* the top ten. Then, collect and add in real-world insights and facts about that job and rinse and repeat if necessary. It won't take long to finalize your job bank into your fully vetted top ten best right fits. For most students, the original top ten stays the top ten because you have already collected a substantial amount of information about each job based on your own good research. Or, you may learn something that will bring one or two or even three or four of your next-highest-scoring jobs into your top ten. You will see how this plays out in Sam's final outcome. And don't worry, I'm going to give you some very good tips about how to collect this real-world information right now—you don't have to go it alone.

A Final Layer of Accuracy: Real World, Real People

Real-world information informs decisions because it's derived from insights and facts provided by *real* people. Adding a final layer of accuracy from those who work or have worked in these exact environments allows you to further ensure that your top ten Working *You* fits are truly right for you. It's really about taking the guesswork out of the career decision-making process as much as possible.

To begin, I strongly encourage you to go back and look closely at what you wrote about your own unique meaning of success in chapter 5. Use this definition as the lens through which you evaluate the real-world information you collect about each job. To help you do this, I'm going to ask you to summarize what success means to you (as Cara and Sam did in their templates at the end of this chapter) before you begin scoring and collecting real-world information. I want you to remember why you are looking for a job and what you want *work you love* to provide in your life. I've found that it adds inspiration and motivation for my own students as they use this information from real people for maximum value.

I hesitate to call this *networking*, because networking can be such a dreaded word, but that's really what it is. Yes, you have to reach out to strangers, and that can sound awkward and scary, but it's also exciting because it has the potential to help you find that first job you love after college. You also might meet a mentor (or two) who will become an invaluable career resource for you years into the future. And you might be surprised to find out that these supposed strangers are more familiar and closely associated with you than you might have imagined. All of these are outcomes my own students have experienced through this last step, and you will likely experience them too. Here are some things to remember as you embark on this effort that I hope will make the process both enjoyable and stress-free:

1. You don't have to be anybody but yourself, so there's no need to fake it—*you are valuable.*
2. Be honest at all times about why you want to talk to someone and where you're at in your own career discovery process—*that makes you likable.*
3. Have fun and make friends—this makes the world livable and enjoyable.

When it comes to collecting real-world information, I want you to become an *information seeker.* You honestly don't want to reach out wearing the hat of a job seeker at this point. Think of it this way: there's nothing you want from any potential contact except their brainpower. Asking people about their expertise and how they got where they are in their careers will likely be received as flattering and satisfying. Wearing the hat of an information seeker instead of a job seeker takes the pressure off—for you and also for them. Why? Because you aren't asking for anything that would typically be considered a tangible commodity, like money or a job. What are they going to say no to? The fact that you think they're successful and knowledgeable?

Typically, when we're approached by people asking us for something tangible, again whether it's money, a job, or even a favor, our first instinct is often to step away. But when we're approached by someone who simply wants to hear what we have to say because they think we're smart, interesting, or have walked a path that they admire—well, we typically take a step *toward* that person. And in this case, that person will be you.

My best advice: Don't automatically send your resume (unless they ask); simply reach out to each person with the goal of getting real-world insights and facts about each job. Think of it as an opportunity to learn how you can set yourself up to live your best life. Tell them why you're reaching out. Tell them that you are trying to fully vet the realities of the employers you are interested in. You can even tell them you've done your research and their company landed on your top ten list of right-fit jobs.

To make reaching out to people you don't know more like reaching out to friends, I want you to leverage connections you already have—like a shared alma mater or even friends of people already in your existing network. *It's going to be fine.*

Find Your Friends

At the risk of sounding like I own stock in LinkedIn (I do not, unfortunately), you are once again going to take another dip into this online well of opportunity.

Let's say Intel is a company in your top ten list of right fits. First, enter the company name into the search box to find a link to the company's profile page. When you get there, you'll see a link that says something like "See all 138,038 employees on LinkedIn" (that's the number of employees at Intel who are on LinkedIn, last time I searched). Once you click on the link, you'll see an "All Filters" icon that allows you to slice and dice all 138,038 Intel employees in a multitude of ways relevant to the functional area, job title, and location you are targeting, as well as any alumni from your alma mater who are associated with the company. If you are a graduate student pursuing your advanced degree at a different institution from where you did your undergraduate work, use both alma maters in your search for connections.

For example, I sliced into the 138,038 Intel employees using my own alma mater, the University of Southern California. Now I'm down to just 946 employees. Depending on the size of the company and the number of alumni from your alma mater, this will of course vary. Nonetheless, you only need one good contact to make a difference. What's the purpose of identifying alumni? The connection you share with other graduates from your own college or university represents what people in my field call a *communication bridge*. It's a common bond that already exists between you and a potential new friend that makes creating a connection much easier and much less stressful.

Also, see what level of LinkedIn connection you have to people at the companies represented in your top ten list or, if you are feeling very ambitious, for all twenty-five jobs in your job bank. For example, if you have a second-level connection, see who you have in common and think about reaching out to the in-common person to see if they might make a connection for you. *Leverage your existing network as you expand it.* As big as the world is, you will quickly discover that the world is smaller than you imagined.

Everything I have discussed here is currently accessible for free on LinkedIn. Also available for free is the opportunity to sort by job titles. You can even enter specific hierarchical levels, such as assistant manager, manager, director, and so on, into the job title box. If you happen to have a paid subscription, you have even more opportunities to slice and dice the data, but the free membership currently gives you all you need to accomplish your goal in this last step.

In addition to communicating on LinkedIn, let everyone know about your interest in the specific companies in your top ten list or, again, all twenty-five jobs in your job bank. Because it's indeed a small world, you might be surprised to find that the least likely person in your existing network *knows someone you need to know.* Definitely use your social media networks to do outreach, and be specific: let your contacts know, for example, that you are interested in learning more about the companies on your list and that you would like to talk to people who work there. You can post your message on Instagram, Facebook, Snapchat, Twitter, or wherever you have a presence.

Also, make sure you tap into the networks of all of the student organizations you belong to, as well as any special interest, religious, or sports groups—basically anyplace in your life where you associate with other people. The worst thing that can happen is that someone will say they don't know anyone. However, based on the experience of all of my students, you'll be surprised who has a friend or relative that you actually need to know.

Getting Started

Start with the largest companies on your top ten list of right fits, because the likelihood that someone from your alma mater or personal networks will have a contact there is greater simply because they employ more people. It's definitely the low-hanging-fruit approach, but it's encouraging to have some good up-front hits as you get into the rhythm of gathering real-world information. Here are a few communication examples to help you reach out.

E-mails to an alumnus from your college or university:

Dear Mr. Benz,

I'm currently a sophomore at Haverford College majoring in economics with a minor in culture and society. I am very interested in learning more about Hulu, because it's at the top of my list as I research and explore career paths that will be a right fit after I graduate.

I'm very impressed by the company and am specifically interested in learning more about the work you do leading Hulu's Originals and Marketing Social division. I've done a lot of research on my own, but getting firsthand information about the realities of this potential career path would be invaluable.

I promise to be very prepared and only take a limited amount of your valuable time. I also noticed that in your LinkedIn profile, we were both on champion tennis teams in high school! Thank you for considering my request.

Best regards,
Cara

Dear Sheri,

I found your profile through the San Diego State University portal on LinkedIn. I'm currently a senior at SDSU and have been doing research on companies I want to work for after graduation. It certainly sounds like you have been very successful at William Blair, and I'm hoping you might find a half hour to share some career advice and insights because I am also pursuing opportunities in investment banking and financial services. Thank you in advance for your consideration!

Best regards,
Sam

Once you've made a connection and set up a time to talk, here are some questions you might ask to help you take away the most useful information possible and make sure you have correctly scored the strength of each fit point. *Focus on how your three You Points will be valued by this employer.* Do your best to learn insights and facts about the employer's Company Character and the Success Factors associated with the type of role you are interested in while further exploring its External Identity. Ask your contacts about their own fit and how their own unique interests and abilities have factored into their success. Here are some example questions.

To learn about Company Character:

- How does your personality fit with the personality of the company?
- What do you like most about the culture or character of the company?
- What role does equity play in the company culture relative to how people are rewarded?
- What have you experienced to be guiding principles for the organization? For example, transparency, ethics, bottom-line-driven, etc.
- How are employees evaluated at the company?

To learn about Success Factors:

- What talents do you feel you bring to the table that have fueled your success?
- What would you say are the ideal skills the company is looking for in this type of role?
- Does the company provide professional development opportunities like mentorship programs or classes to help employees gain new skills?
- My top three talents are [fill in your talents]. How do you see this fitting into this role?
- What talents and skills do you believe have fueled your boss or your boss's boss in their roles at the company?

To learn about External Identity:

- What makes you proudest when you tell people where you work and what you do?
- Do you believe the company walks the talk relative to its mission statement and the values presented on its website?

- What do you most admire about the company's leadership?
- Do you see any changes happening regarding the company's vision for the future?
- Do you think there is a difference between the perception people on the outside have of the company and the experience of those on the inside?

To maximize your experience as you connect with people, take handwritten notes and then enter them into a rolling Word document summarizing your takeaways from each interview. List the date you spoke with the individual, their name and title, and some key insights and facts that speak to the Employer Points for that job. Make sure you also list the date you followed up with a thank-you e-mail or note. This will keep you organized.

Putting It All Together

So let's recap how to put your top ten list of best right fits together, finalize it, and then verify its accuracy with real-world information from real people:

1. Score your twenty-five jobs in your job bank based on the great research you've already done on your own, assigning a 1 to 5 numerical score (5 being the highest) for the strength of each of the three fit points for each job.
2. Add up the three numbers for each job and rank them from one through twenty-five. Begin to reach out to people for real-world information for your top ten best right fits.
3. If you find new insights and facts that change the scoring of any fit point, make the change and recalibrate. If the final score for any of your top ten right fits falls below the score of jobs ranked eleven to twenty-five, pull up that next-highest-scoring job. Recalibrate until you finalize your top ten, which may actually remain the same. I find that even for those students who may make a few changes, the best part is that now you have an inside connection in a field and company that you identified as interesting, and people do change companies. You may impress them, and they'll remember you in a positive way. Who knows, maybe you'll even want to hire *them* in the future!

Ranking Template: Cara

Below is a list of Cara's top ten best right fits, along with her final Working *You* score assigned to each job. You will see that her scores ranged from a final tally of 14 to 15. I find that the top ten for most students fall within a range of 13 to 15, often with many ties, just like Cara. If you would like to see the built-out scoring for all of her twenty-five jobs, you can view or download them at kirksnyder.com.

Netflix: Social Media Assistant Manager, Employer Branding
Fit Point One: 5 + Fit Point Two: 5 + Fit Point Three: 5 = Total Score: 15

Hulu: Associate, Originals Marketing and Social
Fit Point One: 5 + Fit Point Two: 5 + Fit Point Three: 5 = Total Score: 15

LinkedIn: Business Leadership Program Associate
Fit Point One: 5 + Fit Point Two: 5 + Fit Point Three: 5 = Total Score: 15

Shazam: Account Executive
Fit Point One: 5 + Fit Point Two: 5 + Fit Point Three: 4.5 = Total Score: 14.5

Spotify: Client Solutions
Fit Point One: 4.5 + Fit Point Two: 5 + Fit Point Three: 5 = Total Score: 14.5

Cengage: Marketing Coordinator
Fit Point One: 4.5 + Fit Point Two: 5 + Fit Point Three: 4.5 = Total Score: 14

Intuit: Associate Marketing Manager, Social Media & Advertising
Fit Point One: 4.5 + Fit Point Two: 5 + Fit Point Three: 4.5 = Total Score: 14

Nike: Global Membership and Consumer Knowledge Program
Fit Point One: 4.5 + Fit Point Two: 5 + Fit Point Three: 4.5 = Total Score: 14

Tempus: Partner Operations Coordinator
Fit Point One: 5 + Fit Point Two: 4.5 + Fit Point Three: 4.5 = Total Score: 14

YouTube: Coordinator, Creative Partnerships
Fit Point One: 5 + Fit Point Two: 4 + Fit Point Three: 5 = Total Score: 14

Ranking Template: Sam

Sam's top ten list of best right fits ranged from a score of 13 to 15. Sam did have to recalibrate. In his original self-scoring, NASA scored 13.5 and MSNBC scored 13. When he connected to contacts (one alum from his alma mater and one who happened to be a first-level contact with a best friend from high school), he rescored these two jobs based on how he assessed the fit after adding in new insights and facts. They both ended up dropping out of his original top ten ranking. What you see below reflects his pulling both LYFE Marketing and YouTube into his recalibrated top ten list.

Bread: Product Analyst
Fit Point One: 5 + Fit Point Two: 5 + Fit Point Three: 5 = Total Score: 15

William Blair: Analyst
Fit Point One: 5 + Fit Point Two: 5 + Fit Point Three: 5 = Total Score: 15

Loop Capital: Investment Analyst
Fit Point One: 5 + Fit Point Two: 5 + Fit Point Three: 5 = Total Score: 15

Precision Strategies: Mobilization and Campaign Associate
Fit Point One: 5 + Fit Point Two: 5 + Fit Point Three: 5 = Total Score: 15

William Blair: Research Associate
Fit Point One: 5 + Fit Point Two: 4 + Fit Point Three: 5 = Total Score: 14

NBC Universal: Associate, Corporate Strategy and Development
Fit Point One: 5 + Fit Point Two: 4 + Fit Point Three: 5 = Total Score: 14

Blue Origin: Operations Strategist
Fit Point One: 4.5 + Fit Point Two: 4.5 + Fit Point Three: 5 = Total Score: 14

Elected Congressional Official: Congressional Aide
Fit Point One: 4.5 + Fit Point Two: 4 + Fit Point Three: 5 = Total Score: 13.5

LYFE Marketing: Social Media Specialist
Fit Point One: 4.5 + Fit Point Two: 4.5 + Fit Point Three: 4.5 = Total Score: 13.5

YouTube: Development Associate, YouTube Originals
Fit Point One: 4.5 + Fit Point Two: 4 + Fit Point Three: 4.5 = Total Score: 13

Check In . . .

As you begin to create a final blueprint to turn your right fits into job offers, think of yourself as a storyteller. The story is all about you and your future, and you have the opportunity to determine the outcome. Let go of any preconceived ideas about barriers. Ground yourself in the idea that the immense value you bring to the right employer will drive you to your definition of success. Now your story needs a plan. Let's put it together.

11

Turning Right Fits into Job Offers

"A goal without a plan is just a wish."
—Antoine de Saint-Exupéry

Antoine de Saint-Exupéry was a French writer, aviator, and aristocrat, and the recipient of many of France's highest literary awards as well as the US National Book Award. If you've ever taken a classics or literature course, you may have read his most famous book, *The Little Prince*. I chose this quote for our last chapter because Saint-Exupéry, someone who accomplished many goals in what was actually a very short lifetime, recognized that without an effective plan, a goal can easily become an unrealized dream. Plans have a way of making those dreams real. Consider that when Bill Gates held the title of Microsoft chairman, he separated himself from the rest of the world twice a year for what he called Think Week, a time when he immersed himself in technology, literature, and the latest innovations in his field. This was also a time when he planned for the future of his company.

A good plan makes a difference, and for our goal of finding work you love, a good plan provides structure to your story of success. Consider the following: according to Schwab Investor Services, if you poll the top 10 percent of individual performers in the Modern Wealth Index around the world, you'll find that three out of four people in the top 10 percent of wealth—not only in the United States but around the world—have a written plan they follow in order to achieve their financial goals. That's exactly what this final chapter gives you: a written blueprint that is tailor-made for you to turn your right fits into job offers. It's the final step to joining that happy group of new graduates who love their job. The more the merrier, right?

Whether you're a freshman, sophomore, junior, or senior, in a graduate program or have already graduated, it's important that your blueprint has a timeline to frame it. In addition to a timeline, effective plans also have a final goal and benchmarks along the way. And a *really* effective plan has action items to make all the benchmarks achievable, which creates accountability and makes it easy to stay on course. Your blueprint to a job you love includes all of these plan essentials, so let's start with your timeline.

Step 1: Determine the Timeline

If you have one year or less until graduation, you've already graduated, or you're a recent graduate and working in a job that's not a right fit, your timeline will start today and focus on turning your right fits into offers now. If you are a freshman, sophomore, or junior, or are in a graduate program with more than a year to go, your timeline will also start today, but for now will focus on becoming as competitive as possible to turn your right fits into offers when you reach the one-year mark leading up to graduation.

For those of you who are very close to graduating or have already graduated, I recommend that you use a minimum six-month timeline for constructing your blueprint. Your timeline needs to give you enough lead time to feasibly reach your final goal. While one year is ideal, six months is definitely achievable. I've had students who had already graduated go through each of the Working *You* steps and receive an offer in as little as two months. The best advice I can give you is don't judge yourself based on anyone else's timeline.

Leo Tolstoy, regarded as one of the greatest authors of all time, once said, "The two most powerful warriors are patience and time." I want you to regard your timeline not as an adversary to beat or as a source of pressure, but simply as a marathon pacer to keep you from falling out of the race. Cultivate patience and a healthy bit of personal forgiveness as you move forward toward your final goal.

Step 2: Set Your Final Goal

For all timelines, the final goal is you accepting an offer for a job that is meaningful, motivational, and strongly connected to your unique value. This is the outcome of your story—work you love. For example, Cara expressed her final goal as a current sophomore (repeated in her template at the end of this chapter) like this:

"I want to receive my liberal arts degree and have accepted a job offer for one of my top ten right fits. My goal is to have an offer from a company that provides me with the opportunity to succeed based on who I am without feeling as though I have to create a separate work identity to be successful. I know this is going to be extremely important to my happiness and my well-being. My other goal is to make sure this job leverages what I view as my strongest talents: being detail-oriented, a good communicator, and a logical problem solver. I want to feel proud of myself at the end of the day and that my job is taking me where I want to go in my life."

Be as general or specific as you like when setting your final goal based on where you are today. This is *your* plan and it should reflect you.

In Sam's final goal, the company and role are specifically identified because, as a senior, he is focused on turning his right fits into offers now. If you, like Cara, have more than a year until graduation, you'll have the opportunity to update your final goal with more specifics when you hit that one-year mark. Here is how Sam expressed his final goal:

"At graduation, I want to have accepted an offer from Bread, my top-ranked company, as a Product Analyst. My goal is to be rewarded for my Human Value and work for a company that values diversity and individuality, is recognized as innovative and even a disrupter in its field, and that is bringing more dignity to consumer finance. Bread meets these goals, and the role of Product Analyst will definitely play to my talents. I also want to have two other offers to choose from out of my top ten right fits to give myself options. I always want to feel that I am living my best life at any given time, and after graduation, that means a job that is allowing me to succeed and grow to whatever level I am able to reach. I want my first job to set me up for that progression. I want to maximize my potential by bringing my best game and best self to work every day. Basically, I want to be excited about the future and proud of myself for being right where I am at graduation."

Step 3: Establish Benchmarks and Action Items

Once you have determined the duration of your timeline (six months, one year, two years, and so on) and identified your timeline's final goal, you are ready to begin mapping out how you'll get there by establishing periodic benchmarks. Think of benchmarks as subgoals along your timeline to help you proceed at the right speed and stay on your path. The idea being that when you put all of the benchmarks together in the right order, along with action items to make them happen, these benchmarks will take you to the destination of your final goal.

So, let's go into a little more detail about implementing your benchmarks in just the right way, uniquely for you. For example, if you're just starting your sophomore year and have approximately two years before you hit the one-year mark to graduation (like Cara), the first two years of your timeline will be focused on becoming as competitive as possible for your right-fit jobs. Until you reach that one-year countdown, divide your timeline into seasons with a benchmark assigned to each season. For example, a benchmark or subgoal for the summer between your sophomore and junior years might be to have an internship at one of your top ten right fits. Then, backing up, the preceding spring benchmark would include the groundwork that needs to take place in order to secure that summer internship. I will show you how to do this later in the chapter.

Once you hit that one-year countdown to graduation, your focus will change to turning your right fits into offers and updating your final goal with specifics. Along with this change in focus, the timing or pacing of your benchmarks will also change and become less spread out. I suggest that you create benchmarks every month rather than every season. By placing your benchmarks closer together, you create greater purpose and focus on achieving your final goal, and it also provides a welcome by-product: less stress. If you've mapped out what to do and when to do it, it's a lot easier to pace yourself and minimize the hand-wringing, and instead cross the finish line with your hands raised in victory.

So whether your current focus is on becoming as competitive as possible for your right-fit jobs or turning them into offers now, I want you to begin by creating the narrative of your final goal, just like Cara did as a sophomore and

Sam did as a senior. The blueprint won't work if you don't identify a final destination. Think about what you want that finish line to look like and write it down. Craft it. Edit it. Live with it and revise it. Write the outcome of your story in your way, but start with your destination before creating your benchmarks. Knowing where you're going will impact how your story plays out along the way to your final goal.

Building Your Benchmarks

If you have more than one year until graduation and your focus is on becoming as competitive as possible for your best right fits, you will only complete your benchmarks up to that one-year countdown (see Cara's template, page 195). If you are ready to turn your right fits into offers now, complete all of your benchmarks along your timeline. Here's why this approach makes the most sense, particularly for freshmen and sophomores with two or three years until the pivot point. Your personal and professional development between now and that one-year mark to graduation may change some of the rankings in your job bank as you focus on making yourself as competitive as possible. Based on your own development, you may discover new value for yourself, such as new motivational work triggers or new talents. At that one-year mark, I encourage you to revisit your extras list to see if anything at any level (field, company, role) has become *more* interesting than originally scored. This potential recalibration will in turn impact how you update your final goal and help you identify the benchmarks in the last phase of your blueprint as your focus shifts to getting offers now. A good plan is a fully relevant plan, and you don't want to complete your last benchmarks to turn right fits into offers until you're actually ready to implement them. You will see each focus represented in Cara and Sam's blueprints to bring this distinction to life for you.

What I've found to be most effective when creating and setting benchmarks for either focus is to sketch them out along your individual timeline and then stand back and look at them. What order makes the most sense? For example, if your current focus is to become as competitive as possible for your right-fit jobs, a benchmark might be to take an elective class where you are building skills based on specific talents that you know will be leveraged in your top three best right fits. Cara has this in her blueprint. Once you have sketched out all of the benchmarks, visualize how hitting each one in a particular order will effectively take you where you want to go. There's no exact science here, and I encourage you to make any edits, even as your timeline unfolds in real time, that make sense to you in your own life. Think of this as a living document.

Building Your Action Items

Once you have all of your benchmarks in a logical order, it's time to add action items to make it all happen. Action items are simply bullet points under each benchmark that make up your to-do list—actions you can take in order to hit each benchmark. Action items are guardrails that help you stay on course, remain accountable to your goal, and further customize your plan. Each bullet point gives you instructions for taking action. They make your plan attainable, because you never have to think *What do I need to do next?*

For example, here are the first three benchmarks along with action items for Sam, who is just beginning his senior year, so his timeline is spaced out month by month and, again, focused on turning his top ten right fits into offers now:

Benchmark #1

September, Senior Year: Network into my top ten right fits, focusing on Bread as my number one choice. Refine my communication skills for an interview based on why I believe I'm a right fit for these jobs. Begin to submit resumes as I identify available right-fit jobs.

Action Items:

- Do information interviews to make new contacts at Bread and the other companies in my top ten.
- Search the websites of each company in my top ten and look for job listings that align with my list.
- Begin the formal application process for all available right-fit jobs.
- Get feedback on my resume from the career center as well as professors and professionals in my right fields to make sure it is in the best shape possible.

- Do mock job interviews and get feedback from advisors in the career center about my interviewing skills.
- Practice telling my story about why I believe I'm a right fit for the job. Record myself and assess how I answer the "Tell me about yourself" question.

Benchmark #2

October, Senior Year: Continue to focus my energies on creating contacts and finding opportunities at Bread and my other top ten right fits, but also revisit other jobs in my job bank to see if I need to or want to further explore any of these as backups, based on who is hiring when I graduate next May. Develop skills that will make me competitive for these jobs.

Action Items:

- Hold myself accountable to following up with a thank-you e-mail or handwritten note after each information or job interview to create a positive impression.
- Review the Working *You* fit points for each job and remind myself why I'm a right fit for each of these roles and why I deserve to be there.
- Reach out to three new people each week.
- Take on a role in a student organization to develop leadership and strategy skills.
- Begin and/or continue the formal application process for all available right-fit jobs.

Benchmark #3

November, Senior Year: Zero in on what my other preferred jobs outside of Bread are and make a concentrated effort to apply for right roles in each of these companies. Network and interview.

Action Items:

- Follow up with any contacts relevant to my search at any of my preferred companies.
- Research the marketplace for each of my top ten companies (or top twenty-five) and look at the hiring expectations or any innovations that might lead to new opportunities.
- Continue to reach out to three new people each week.
- Attend any information sessions or company events relevant to my search that are held by the career center.
- Assess my performance in any interviews and personally follow up with all interviewers.
- Examine my next three benchmarks and make any necessary adjustments.

Facing Challenges

Time and again my students tell me that once they start putting their blueprint together, it begins to write itself. Just dive into it. What I most enjoy hearing is that, after it's completed, students typically find a new sense of security about their future. Having a plan puts you in control. Having direction is a good thing. Remember, you've done all of the heavy lifting; now you're simply making your successful future and final goal a reality. As the opening quote implies, having a plan is what makes wishes come true.

Does everything always go smoothly? Will your plan guarantee that all falls into place? It would be dishonest to say yes. We all know that everything doesn't always go as perfectly as planned. At the beginning of this chapter I noted that three out of four people in the top 10 percent of wealth in the world have a written plan they follow to achieve their financial goals. It's safe to say that even for those billionaires with great financial plans, there are still unexpected economic, political, human, and even natural-world influences that can have negative impacts. A thoughtful and carefully built plan becomes even more important in times of uncertainty or unexpected challenges because it prevents you from getting sidetracked and stuck.

So let's say that none of the jobs on your top ten list are available when you're ready to turn your right fits into job offers because these companies simply aren't hiring. Your first goal should always be to get a job you love. But if that isn't possible right now for whatever reason, your second goal should be to get a job that allows you to gain experience relevant to your right fits so you can make a move as soon as the situation changes. This is why your extras list exists—because there will always be factors you can't control.

The Working *You* system is designed to expand your job search horizons, not limit them. As you will see in Sam's blueprint template, there's a built-in opportunity adjustment every three months based on the hiring realities of the marketplace. This includes further exploration of jobs eleven to twenty-five in your job bank and, if necessary, pulling the extras list into play from chapters 7, 8, and 9 to generate additional right fits to explore. These opportunities prevent you from getting sidetracked. But let me be clear, if you find that you need to make adjustments, don't accept less than you deserve. Making adjustments is like going to your favorite ice cream store and discovering that they don't have your favorite flavor. You can still walk away satisfied because some other flavors taste pretty damn good too—and next time, your favorite flavor will likely be back.

Let's use Sam's favorite company, Bread, as an example. And yes, this is a spoiler alert that you will see play out in his own custom blueprint and final story. While he identified the role of Product Analyst to pursue at Bread, that position isn't available. But while investigating and networking, he found a similar role available at Bread that will also reward his Functional Value. Perhaps the Product Manager role didn't initially sound as enjoyable as Product Analyst, but it does sound interesting based on our definition of interesting. The first connection point between Sam's Human Value and the Company Character of Bread hasn't changed at all. These fit points remain locked in because the employer is the same and Sam is the same. The third connection point between Sam's Image Value and the External Identity of the company also stays locked in because, again, both the employer and Sam remain the same. In Sam's case, a different role at a right-fit company prevents him from having to dim his light or look at the ground when people ask him where he works because the first and third points remain locked in. These two fit points are his bedrocks, and pursuing a different role that might not be his first choice but will still leverage his talents and skills at that same company is exactly what those billionaires do when unexpected influences impact their financial plans. They make sound and informed adjustments based on real-world factors, which is exactly what I'm recommending you do too. Yes, it's the real world, and sometimes there are going to be adjustments and trade-offs. So if you have to dig into jobs eleven to twenty- five, pull your extras list into play to create additional right fits, or, like Sam, explore other roles at one of your top ten companies, *go for it*.

On the first page of this book, I told you the reason I believe students get lost in the murky sea of finding work they love seems to be less about the economy flourishing or languishing—and more about understanding how to *systematically connect who you are with what you do* based on the realities of any current job market. The Working *You* system was designed to work under just about any conditions. Being open to adapting your plan because of the realities of the marketplace is key to reaching your final goal. Even if you are facing challenges that require you to take a job mainly to generate cash flow, don't give up on the system. Continue to work your plan and you will avoid getting sidetracked and stuck. Change is a given; bad economic times will eventually give way to good economic times, and you want to be first in line for that job you love. Even when you're facing challenges, you still want to position yourself to join that small, happy group of new graduates and find a job you love.

Now, let's take a look at Cara and Sam's final blueprints and how it played out for them so you can get a better idea about how to write your story. Your blueprint is your own, and different from anyone else's, because your Human Value, Functional Value, and Image Value make you unique. Your definition of success is also unique. Once you get started writing your story, your path to the future will take on a life of its own as you map it out. I believe in you and I believe in your value. *Design your future and get ready to live your best life.*

Final Blueprint Template: Cara

Final Goal: I want to receive my liberal arts degree and have accepted a job offer from one of my top ten right fits. My goal is to have an offer from a company that provides me with the opportunity to succeed based on who I am without feeling as though I have to create a separate work identity to be successful. I know this is going to be extremely important to my happiness and my well-being. My other goal is to make sure this job leverages what I view as my strongest talents: being detail-oriented, a good communicator, and a logical problem solver. I want to feel proud of myself at the end of the day and that my job is taking me where I want to go in my life.

Benchmark #1: Spring (Sophomore Year)
Start getting real facts about the companies I'm interested in and see if the Employer Points really represent what I need in a job. Continue to develop my professional brand.

Action Items:
- Make connections with alumni from Haverford who are working for any of my top ten right fits.
- Find out about any internship opportunities I might be able to pursue next summer between my junior and senior years.
- Look at possible second- and third-level LinkedIn connections at these companies.
- Get resume feedback from the career center and from people doing what I want to do.
- Take a free online seminar or class that's relevant to one or two of my right-fit fields.
- Work on my LinkedIn account.

continued

Benchmark #2: Summer (Between Sophomore and Junior Year)

Take at least one summer class online based on what's available while I'm home for my degree requirements. Earn money! Set up information interviews in person and online. Become more knowledgeable about my top fields.

Action Items:
- Zero in on companies with Chicago offices to learn about their organizational structure.
- Check my social media accounts and make edits to create a more professional appearance for employers.
- Read two classic business books.

Benchmark #3: Fall (Junior Year)

Continue to equip myself with real-world facts from people from my top ten list. Expand my interests and keep my options open.

Action Items:
- Take an elective that will leverage my interests and talents to build skills for jobs on my right-fit top ten list.
- Take advantage of the resources and services at my career center.
- Join professional associations in my field of choice at the student rate (or even better, free) to increase my connections and at the same time gain a competitive advantage over other candidates.
- Continue to network into my top ten companies and get on-the-ground information about these employers from people who work there or have worked there.
- Recalibrate my top ten list if necessary.

Benchmark #4: Winter (Junior Year)

Keep networking and start applying to internships.

Action Items:

- Leverage my connections to get my resume in front of hiring managers for summer internships.
- Practice my interview skills and follow up on my resume submissions.
- Head down and keep believing in myself.
- Go back to my job bank if I need to, because they are all potentially right fits.
- Start interviewing for internships either with the companies on my list or in my job bank, but if location and salary don't make that feasible, then look for relevant internships similar to my identified right fits.

Benchmark #5: Spring (Junior Year)

Secure an internship for the summer and focus on having a successful semester.

Action Items:

- Interview and network.
- Get feedback whenever possible about my resume and interviewing skills.
- Go back to my job bank if I feel I need more options.
- If I have more than one internship opportunity, look at the strength of the fit at each point in the system.
- Focus on my classes.
- Sign up through the career center for any recruiting programs that will be relevant.
- Attend any company nights or career panels at the career center or sponsored by other college centers or organizations that would be important for me to attend.

continued

Benchmark #6: Summer (Between Junior and Senior Years)

Intern and learn—about myself and the field of my internship. Continue to grow as a professional and become more focused about what's going to be the best right fit for me after graduation.

- Use my talents in my internship.
- Get feedback whenever possible and as appropriate about my performance to increase my self-awareness and continue to develop.
- Read a classic business book.
- Read a new business book that's currently on the bestseller list.
- Continue to network into my top ten list and go beyond it into other roles in my job bank—expanding my network and my knowledge about different companies can only be a good thing!
- Revisit my top ten list and my extras list, explore any new fields, companies, and roles that now qualify as interesting, and, based on what I've learned about myself, possibly recalibrate and then pivot to focusing on turning my right fits into job offers now. Complete my benchmarks and action items to reach my final goal.

Note: At this point, Cara will have reached her one-year mark to graduation. She will first recalibrate her job bank, update her final goal, and begin to set benchmarks on a monthly basis instead of seasonally. See a fully built-out blueprint for Cara's last year of college, along with blank templates to build your own custom blueprint, at kirksnyder.com.

Final Blueprint Template: Sam

Note: As a first-semester senior, Sam has built his blueprint around monthly benchmarks because he is ready to turn his right fits into offers.

Final Goal: At graduation, I want to have accepted an offer from Bread, my top-ranked company, as a Product Analyst. My goal is to be rewarded for my Human Value and work for a company that values diversity and individuality, is recognized as innovative and even a disrupter in its field, and that is bringing more dignity to consumer finance. Bread meets these goals, and the role of Product Analyst will definitely play to my talents. I also want to have two other offers to choose from out of my top ten right fits to give myself options. I always want to feel that I am living my best life at any given time, and after graduation that means a job that is allowing me to succeed and grow to whatever level I am able to reach. I want my first job to set me up for that progression. I want to maximize my potential by bringing my best game and best self to work every day. Basically, I want to be excited about the future and proud of myself for being right where I am at graduation.

Benchmark #1: September

Network into my top ten right fits, focusing on Bread as my number one choice. Refine my communication skills for an interview based on why I believe I'm a right fit for these jobs. Begin to submit resumes as I identify available right-fit jobs.

Action Items:
- Do information interviews to make new contacts at Bread and the other companies in my top ten.
- Search the websites of each company in my top ten and look for job listings that align with my list.
- Begin the formal application process for all available right-fit jobs.
- Get feedback on my resume from the career center as well as professors and professionals in my right fields to make sure it is in the best shape possible.

continued

- Do mock job interviews and get feedback from advisors in the career center about my interviewing skills.
- Practice telling my story about why I believe I'm a right fit for the job. Record myself and assess how I answer the "Tell me about yourself" question.

Benchmark #2: October

Continue to focus my energies on creating contacts and finding opportunities at Bread and my other top ten right fits, but also revisit other jobs in my job bank to see if I need to or want to further explore any of these as backups, based on which firms are hiring when I graduate next May. Develop skills that will make me competitive for these jobs.

Action Items:

- Hold myself accountable to following up with a thank-you e-mail or handwritten note after each information or job interview to create a positive impression.
- Review the *Working You* fit points for each job, and remind myself why I'm a right fit for each of these roles and why I deserve to be there.
- Reach out to three new people each week.
- Take on a role in a student organization to develop leadership and strategy skills.
- Begin and/or continue the formal application process for all available right-fit jobs.

Benchmark #3: November

Zero in on my other preferred jobs outside of Bread and make a concentrated effort to apply for right fits in each of these companies. Network and interview.

Action Items:

- Follow up with any contacts relevant to my search at any of my preferred companies.
- Research the marketplace for each of my top ten companies (or top twenty-five) and look at the hiring expectations or any new innovations that might lead to new opportunities.
- Continue to reach out to three new people each week.
- Attend any information sessions or company events at the career center that could be useful to me.
- Assess my performance in any interviews and personally follow up with all interviewers.
- Examine my next three benchmarks and make any needed adjustments/recalibrations.

Benchmark #4: December

Keep networking. Keep interviewing. Enjoy the holidays with my friends and family.

Action Items:

- Revisit my three Value Points and remind myself why I'd be valuable to my employer. Use them as the foundation of my interview to communicate why I'm the right candidate for the job.
- Update my LinkedIn profile and resume to reflect my latest and greatest.
- Check to see if there are any other alumni from SDSU who might have recently joined any companies where I'm applying for jobs.
- Let any networking contact I've made at the companies where I'm interviewing know that I have an interview. Keep them updated.
- Talk to my family about my job search!

continued

Benchmark #5: January

Connect, interview, and get offers. Recalibrate my job bank and blueprint as necessary for the remaining benchmarks until graduation.

Action Items:

- Sleep, take care of myself, and keep moving forward on my path.
- Organize my schedule and stay on top of who I've talked to and where I am in the process for each job.
- Follow up if I haven't heard back.
- Send thank-you correspondence to all of my interviewers within twenty-four hours of the interview.
- Check in with my career center for advice about following up and negotiating offers.
- Sleep, take care of myself, and keep moving forward on my path! (Bookended this one!)

Benchmark #6: February

If I've made any recalibration, move forward and don't give up. Keeping this benchmark simple and focused!

Action Items:

- Put in the time.
- Seek out mentors and surround myself with people who believe in my goals.
- Be willing to fail, and don't see failure as an ending. Pick myself up and keep going, because I count.
- Review the value I bring to the job market and keep it close.
- Examine my remaining benchmarks and make any needed adjustments/recalibrations. Commit to a strong finish for the semester and my college career.

Benchmark #7: March

Interview with companies I have reached out to and also explore job listings for all of the companies in my job bank to expand my opportunities without sacrificing my Functional Value. Also, look at the job listings for similar companies and create a Working *You* score for any job that qualifies as interesting based on the field, company, and role. Planning to hedge my bet here and cover all bases!

Action Items:
- Explore new opportunities.
- Send out resumes and network, focusing on SDSU alumni as a first step into interesting companies.
- Enjoy my last spring break! I decided to put this into my blueprint because it's *my* blueprint, and I think it's important!

Benchmark #8: April

I'm targeting to reach my final goal early. Hopefully, this is where I have a mic-drop moment.

Action Items:
- Follow through.
- Bring my best self to every interview.
- Accept an offer from an employer I believe in and that will reward me for the value I bring to the job.

continued

Benchmark #9: May

Reach Final Goal: At graduation, I want to have accepted an offer from Bread, my top-ranked company, as a Product Analyst. My goal is to be rewarded for my Human Value and work for a company that values diversity and individuality, is recognized as innovative and even a disrupter in its field, and that is bringing more dignity to consumer finance. Bread meets these goals, and the role of Product Analyst will definitely play to my talents. I also want to have two other offers to choose from out of my top ten right fits to give myself options. I always want to feel that I am living my best life at any given time, and after graduation that means a job that is allowing me to succeed and grow to whatever level I am able to reach. I want my first job to set me up for that progression. I want to maximize my potential by bringing my best game and best self to work every day. Basically, I want to be excited about the future and proud of myself for being right where I am at graduation.

Action Items:
- If I do not have an offer . . . stay committed, stay focused, and stay connected to all potential opportunities. Dig into my extras list and create new right-fit job options if I need to. Remind myself that there is more than one right-fit job out there, and I only need one.

The Reality for Cara and Sam

As I mentioned early on when I introduced Cara and Sam as student models, they are composites of thousands of undergraduate and graduate students I have had in my classes or interviewed specifically for this book. Nonetheless, they too have endings to their stories. Of course, as student models their outcomes are best described as *likely outcomes*, but these are very much based on the real-life twists and turns experienced by the students they bring to life along this same path. So to help you better envision the possibilities of your own happy outcome, I'm sharing where Cara and Sam landed in their respective journeys toward finding jobs they love.

Cara's Story

Cara approached and implemented her plan as you would expect someone who describes herself as goal-driven and results-focused would. Because she was a first-semester sophomore when she completed her custom blueprint and had almost two years before pivoting to turn her right fits into job offers, she was focused on becoming as competitive as possible for her identified best right fits.

The first thing she did after completing her blueprint was to reach out and have conversations with two contacts she found on LinkedIn. One worked at Netflix and the other at Hulu—and both were in Los Angeles. One was an alumnus from Haverford and another was a cold call who, she learned from the profile, had also been a champion tennis player in high school. This was a commonality that Cara shared in her request for an informational interview. Both connections were valuable, and Cara believed she had correctly assessed the strength of the fit between her Human Value and Company Character as well as her Image Value and External Identity for both Netflix and Hulu. Through her conversation with her contact from Netflix, Cara heard something new about the Success Factors of the Netflix role that resonated. As a result, she decided to take a spring elective focused on social media and brand identity.

Spring brought new connections and more informational interviews that covered most of her top ten right-fit jobs. Cara found that she loved her elective class, which further confirmed she would have the wind at her back in a role similar to the identified Netflix role. During the summer between her sophomore and junior years, she connected with the brother of a friend from college who works at Spotify, which was ranked number five on her top ten list. Through this new contact, Cara was able to set up an in-person meeting with two professionals at Spotify in Chicago, Cara's hometown and where she was planning to spend the summer working for her aunt's real estate company. When she went into Spotify, she was prepared. She talked about why she was interested in the company, and why she thought she was likely a right fit for a marketing role. The meeting confirmed what she had learned about the company and the role, and she got along really well with the people she met. Even though it was mid-June, they unexpectedly offered her a six-week internship because she impressed them as being motivated and engaged—and a right fit. After a fast conversation with her aunt, she got the okay to bow out of her summer job, and quickly accepted the internship at Spotify. The internship was a success, and she left thinking she would love to work there after graduation.

Cara's junior year was spent continuing to build skills that leveraged her talents; she also connected with the career center and began to access all of the university's career resources. She continued to follow up with all of the networking contacts she had previously made, and through the career center's recruiting program, interviewed for a summer internship at Salesforce. Cara had actually identified a job at Salesforce in her job bank, and even though it didn't make her top ten, it was still a right fit. The internship focused on product marketing, a different role than she had identified, but it would allow her to work cross-functionally across product management and sales to strategically drive new initiatives. The internship was part of their Futureforce program, and when she recalibrated her job bank with this new role, she found that it scored on par with the jobs in her top ten list of best right fits. She was able to do the internship in Chicago, which was perfect, because living at home and not paying rent was the doable option.

At the beginning of her senior year, it was time to pivot to turning right-fit jobs into offers now. She was smart to stay in touch with everyone she had worked with at Spotify the previous summer as well as her other contacts. Cara decided that she wanted to start her career in her hometown of Chicago and began to focus on right fits there.

Leveraging her network, including her past supervisors at both Spotify and Salesforce, she reached out to her greater network and let everyone know she was ready to seek employment as soon as she graduated in May. She realized that her Chicago focus took both Netflix and Hulu out of play, but she also knew location was an important part of her right fit. Three weeks into the start of her last semester, Cara had two solid offers for employment from Spotify and Salesforce (both in Chicago), and she was down to the last interview with a large finance company that she was also pursuing through her university's recruiting program. There were two other jobs in the mix as well. One was on her original top ten list, and another just recently emerged with a very new start-up marketing firm that she added to her job bank in the fall when she had updated and recalibrated. She was also getting down to the final interview for the start-up.

Finding Work You Love

Admittedly, her head was spinning a bit about which job was going to be the best job, but she was reminded by a mentor that as long as they were all categorized as right fits, even if there were small degrees of difference, there wasn't a bad choice. By mid-February, both Spotify and Salesforce needed an answer, and Cara then took herself out of the running for the start-up because, as a "calculated risk taker," the thought of taking a risk on what was still a *very new* start-up wasn't a risk she felt was worth taking. Cara also looked back at her own unique definition of success, and realized that growth and making money without being stressed out about the stability of her next paycheck was the right thing to do.

At the end of February, Cara accepted the Salesforce role in product marketing, and will be working for the same manager she worked for successfully as an intern the previous summer. What she liked most about her new boss at Salesforce was the regular check-ins and how employees were recognized for their contributions. As a bonus, she also loved the aesthetics of the office! Cara was very smart in handling her other potential employers in an honest way, making sure not to string them along and be anything less than professional. She found that she had actually put together a pretty substantial network through all of her informational interviews and internships, which she knew would serve her well in her life after graduation. Cara reached her blueprint's original final goal: a job that allowed her to succeed based on who she is in the world while leveraging her key talents, and was off on her own path in her hometown of Chicago.

Sam's Story

Sam did all the right things. He followed his plan, and true to his personality and talents—being strategic, goal-driven, and determined—he fully leveraged the alumni network from San Diego State University and immediately began to network into his top companies. He made some strong connections right away and received good information as well as advice about refining his resume to target several of his specific companies when one of his connections requested that he send his resume. He also found that his original assessments of the fit for each job were for the most part on target.

He had three early interviews before December of his senior year: one at NBC Universal, one at YouTube, and one Skype interview with William Blair.

At the end of January, he was starting to feel anxious when he learned that a handful of companies in his top ten simply weren't going to be hiring. So, just as he'd built into his plan at benchmark #6, he recalibrated his job bank and pulled into play several other possibilities from outside of his top ten. By mid-February he had another interview with NBC Universal, and even though he was getting very positive feedback, he continued to network, apply for available opportunities, and stay focused. At the end of February, he received a call from the technology company Bread. He had ranked it as a perfect 15 but had pretty much given up hope about hearing back, although he had traded a couple of e-mails with contacts he'd made through LinkedIn. As things often happen when it is a right fit, the interview process moved fast. What he learned, however, was that the job he had been interested in, Product Analyst, wasn't available. Although his heart sank when he heard that voice-mail message from the company, there was another job that *was* going to be available, that of Product Manager. It wasn't something that had been on his radar; if it had been, he'd likely have scored it much as he had the Product Analyst role, because it also fully leveraged his talents. Meanwhile, the interview process at two other companies began, while other potential employers told him no thanks. By the end of April, Sam had turned down two offers and accepted the offer at Bread as a Product Manager. And yes, Sam had a great time at graduation and reached his final goal of having an accepted offer from Bread in an inclusive environment where he is allowed to succeed and grow to whatever level he is able to reach.

Check In . . .

You did it. You are on your way to joining that happy group of new college graduates who love their job. Welcome to that gateway we talked about in the introduction, where people who love their jobs live their professional lives. Nicely done! Your goals are no longer simply wishes. You have a custom blueprint to *implement* your goals. Implementation turns wishes into realities—*your reality.* Recognize your tremendous accomplishment of taking action and taking ownership over your career and your future. *Yes, you have a plan. Yes, you are on your path to success. Bravo.* I'll see you in the conclusion for a lifetime of Working *You.*

Conclusion

A Lifetime of Working *You*

*"You can only become truly accomplished
at something you love."*
—Maya Angelou

It's true. If you don't love what you do, you won't fully realize your potential. Hopefully, I've given you some new reasons to believe in that potential, along with some strategies to help you put all of your unique value to work doing something you love.

I picked this quote by Maya Angelou to conclude the book for a specific reason. Angelou is widely considered one of the most significant individuals in the twentieth and twenty-first centuries. She faced many adversities in her life but had a wildly successful, five-decade career. During that career she took on many different roles, from singer and dancer to civil rights activist, writer, and poet. The takeaway for you is that in each of these roles, Angelou was extremely accomplished, and from my perspective she succeeded because she loved each role.

The steps in the Working *You* system can be used for making sure each role you take during your very long and successful career is a right fit. All the ingredients that went into discovering and defining each of your individual You Points, as well as the correlating Employer Points of each job in your job bank, can be adapted for any job in your future—even if it represents a completely different field, company, or role. No matter how you evolve or what new doors present themselves, doing your best to make sure each role rewards the unique value you bring to the job market will keep you moving ahead in a productive and positive direction.

You have the ability to accomplish what you desire because the catalyst for reaching success is something you already possess: your value. It's not a pie-in-the-sky sentiment or a lofty goal. I've seen the practical outcome of individual accomplishment when people just like you are intrinsically motivated because they love their job. That happiness is why I went hunting for a system I could share with students who were unemployed, underemployed, or unhappy with their jobs after college. Once you find a right-fit job, I'm willing to bet that you'll never want to accept anything else.

Working *You* into the Future

Earlier in the book, I shared some of the career fears my graduate students expressed. One of the fears I didn't note is an important one I saved until now: "I'm afraid that I'll hate my next job too, and spend the rest of my career trying to find something that doesn't exist." This is a fear that I believe you will never have to face as long as you refuse to accept less than being rewarded for your value at work. You *can* find work you love if you're listening to your own "sounds" and following your own path. Let your Human Value, Functional Value, and Image Value guide you through your career, and use the correlating Employer Points to make sure you're locked in at your first job, second job, and every job thereafter. Being intrinsically motivated because you love what you do is what *Finding Work You Love* is all about.

The Working *You* system has evolved over many years, and includes ideas and principles I have been exploring and writing about for a long time. *But it has evolved.* The danger we all face is getting stuck. Don't settle for stuck. You work hard to get into college and even harder to graduate. That work deserves an outcome worthy of your effort.

If you would like to continue to engage in this conversation about finding work you love, I will be posting new interviews that did not appear in the book that I hope can add further value to your journey. I will also be posting updates and advice from the amazing people who so generously shared their stories with you in these pages at kirksnyder.com. Join me there!

I hope you share this information with your friends and even with your parents. Share it with anyone you feel might benefit from ideas in the book that have resonated with you. A lifetime of Working *You* is my wish for you. I want you to be able to say, *Yes, this is why I went to college. This makes it all worth it!*

About the Author

Kirk Snyder is an award-winning business communication professor at his alma mater, the University of Southern California. His work has been featured in *Time*, *Fast Company*, *Fortune*, and the *New York Times*. He has spoken at some of the world's largest companies on the intersection of communication, culture, and careers in a changing world of work. And his undergraduate and graduate work span business, communication, and organizational change and leadership. He lives in Southern California.

Index

Franklin, Benjamin, 147, 168
friends, networking with, 177–78
Fuller, Garland, 108–9
fun, 128–29
Functional Value
    example of, 18
    importance of, 25
    key attributes of, 22–24
    roles and, 147–48
    Success Factors and, 22, 31, 70, 106, 110
    See also skills; talents

G

Gandhi, Mahatma, 73, 74, 82
Gates, Bill, 185
Gladwell, Malcolm, 125
Glassdoor, 131, 133, 153
Glenn, John, 85
goals
    examples of, 187
    plans and, 185–86
    setting final, 187
Goleman, Daniel, 22
Google, 149
Graham, Martha, 35–36, 41
Grazer, Brian, 149
Gucci Beauty, 130–31

H

Hemingway, Ernest, 57, 72
Hilfman, Ashley, 150–51
Hoffman, Reid, 81
Hofmann, Wilhelm, 75
Huffington, Arianna, 87

Human Value
    Company Character and, 19, 20, 30, 106
    importance of, 19, 21, 35–36, 55
    key attributes of, 19–21, 36
    See also demographics; motivational work triggers; personality

I

Image Value
    examples of, 26–27, 76–77, 79–81
    External Identity and, 26, 31, 75, 82, 107, 109
    importance of, 29, 74, 75, 82
    intrinsic motivation and, 26
    key attributes of, 27–28, 74
    See also ego; reputation
influencers, 35–36, 55
intrinsic motivation
    engagement and, 113–14
    fields and, 117
    Image Value and, 26
    power of, 4–5
introverts, 41, 44, 106

J

job bank
    measuring fit of jobs in, 173–75, 181–83
    uses for, 99
    vetting ranking of jobs in, 173, 175–81
    See also 5-5-1 job-search method
job offers
    examples of, 204–8
    as final goal, 187
    turning right fits into, 99, 185–208
Jung, Carl, 173